Like Sorr

C000081024

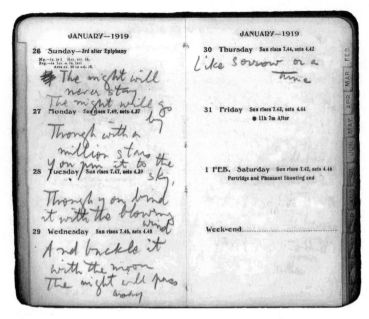

Extract from the 1919 Diary of Eleanor Farjeon
(13th February 1881 - 5th June 1965)

Reproduction of the manuscript of her poem 'The Night Will Never
Stay' with its last line, 'Like sorrow or a tune' which has been taken
as a title for this collection.

Cover Illustration

This is a detail of the dress Eleanor Farjeon is seen wearing in the
photograph on the back cover. In her unpublished memoir, she
wrote about the outfit which she had bought in the Russian shop
Polunins of Bond Street, a shop popular with the lovers of the
Diaghilev Ballet, "My shirt (17/6d in the Summer Sale) was of
handspun linen, so heavy that I needed to wear little else in the hot
weather. I did my gardening in it and have never enjoyed a fashion
so free and simple. It was of natural colour, bound with scarlet tape,
the front embroidered with medallions of bright silk. I wore it with
red or brown stockings and leather sandals, and when I slung on my
rope harness to go wooding I must have looked like something out of
Prince Igor let loose on the Sussex roads. Yet the villagers accepted
me as I was."

LIKE SORROW OR A TUNE

Poems by
ELEANOR FARJEON
A NEW SELECTION

EDITED AND INTRODUCED BY
ANNE HARVEY

WITH A PREFACE BY
PIERS PLOWRIGHT

for Rowan Middleton,
with good wishes,
from
Anne Harvey

4 September
2019 —

LAUREL BOOKS

First published in 2013
by Laurel Books
282 The Common Holt Wiltshire BA14 6QJ

Printed by CPI Antony Rowe Ltd
Bumpers Farm Chippenham Wiltshire SN14 6QA

British Library Cataloguing in Publication Data
A CIP record for this book is available from the British Library

ISBN 978-1873390-14-6

CONTENTS

Preface, by Piers Plowright   ix
Introduction, by Anne Harvey   xii

CHILDHOOD'S FLICKERING SHADOW
Good Morning   3
Waking Up   3
There Isn't Time!   4
The Old Man's Toes   4
Bravery   6
House Coming Down   7
Blind Alley   8
Girls' Names   9
Joan's Corner   9
Meeting Mary   9
Bronwen of the Flowers   10
Myfanwy Among the Leaves   11
For Joan   12
Griselda   12
Hide-And-Seek (Hiding)   14
Hide-And-Seek (Seeking)   15
The Other Child   15
Here We Go Round the Mulberry Bush   16
Boys' Names   17
In Goes Robin   18
Ned   18
Bedtime   19
Good Night   20
A Drink of Water   20
Light The Lamps Up, Lamplighter   21
Oh, Hark!   22
It Was Long Ago   22

THE TIDE IN THE RIVER
The Tide in the River   24
Sonnets from 'First Love'   24
Sonnets from 'Interim'   25
The Reflection   26
Silence   28

I Come to Wish   28
For Shadows   28
Sonnets from 'Second Love' (to Edward Thomas)   29
A Mother to Her Daughter   30
Sonnets from 'Second Love'   30
On the Snow   32
Three Miles to Penn   32
The Outlet   33
Easter Monday (In Memoriam E.T.)   34
Peace   34
The Night Will Never Stay   35

THE GIFT OF ENGLISH WORDS

Alphabet   36
English   36
Mary Indoors   37
Knowledge   38
Latin   38
Ornithology   39
Poetry   40
Mary's One   40
Pegasus   41
Books   42

ROOM FOR ANOTHER ONE

Mrs Malone   44
Cats   48
The Golden Cat   48
Mr Sheraton's Cat   49
To Coney: My Kitten   50
Dog   50
Inside   51
Nothing   52
Epitaph   52

DIVERSIONS

From 'The ABC of the BBC'   53
  B is for Big Ben   53
  J is for Jazz, L is for Licence   54
  N is for News Bulletin   55

P is for Programme   56
 Q is for Questions   57
Preferences   58
Reflections on Two Pins   58
Random Reflections on a Park Seat   59
The Perfection of the Stranger   60
A Lullaby in Lingerie   61
The Immortal Motley   61
Ravenous Justice   62
An Exposure of the Creeps   63
Tree-Law   64
The Dull Side of Things   64
The Game That's Never Done   65
From 'The Town Child's Alphabet'   67
  F is for Flower Seller, J is for Jazz Man   67
  P is for Policeman, Q is for Queue Girl   68
  R is for Roadmender, T is for Taxi-Man, U is for Uncle   69
  W is for Waitress   70
From 'A Sussex Alphabet'   70
  Arundel   70
  Belloc, Long Man of Wilmington, Rye, Uckfield   71
  All the Way to Alfriston   72
From 'Nursery Rhymes of London Town'   73
  King's Cross   73
  The Stock Exchange, Shepherd's Bush, Battersea   74
  Hammersmith, Kensal Rise, The Angel   75
  Fleet Street, Oxford Circus, Wormwood Scrubs   76
  Bloomsbury   76
  Willesden, St. Mary Axe   77
To Ted from Eleanor   78
Serenade to H.G., Thirty Years After   79
Gather Up Your Litter   80

THE GATE IN THE WALL

Morning Light   82
The First Blackbird   82
A Dragonfly   83
Kingfisher   83
Gossamer   84
Kestrel   84

Poppies   85
The White Blackbirds   85
The Garden in the Dark   86
Poplars at Night   86
Evening Hushes   86
Burning the Gate   87
The Gate in the Wall   87

THE ENDING OF THE YEAR

Hallowe'en   89
Now! Says Time   89
The Old Man Sweeps the Leaves   90
The Bonfire   90
The Ending of the Year   91
Thames in December   92
Pledges on the Snow   92
Snowfall   94
The Children's Carol   94
Music at Night   95
Shall I to the Byre Go Down?   95
The Third Joyful Mystery   96
The Song of the Fir   97
The Mother's Tale   98
A Wish   99
The Tired Tree   99

MORNING HAS BROKEN

Morning Has Broken   101
We May Not Say We Love   101
Saturday Night   102
A Prayer   103
One Day   103
To D.B.   104
The Need   105
Perfect Rest   106

Notes   107
Select Bibliography   121
Index of Titles   123

PREFACE

How my sister and I met Eleanor Farjeon might have become the subject of one of her poems: two children, playing at the bottom of their doctor father's Hampstead garden, dared each other to roll over a wall and explore the mysterious kingdom beyond where they found, sitting on a chair under an apple tree, not a witch, but a benign old woman (she seemed *very* old to us) with huge glasses and a warm smile who invited us in for tea. This must have been about 1948, the first of many enchanted visits. There was a cat, there were intriguing books heaped on and around collapsing chairs, there was often another guest who seemed nearly as fascinating as she was – the actor and great friend Denys Blakelock – and there were the stories: walking with Edward Thomas whom she loved so deeply and hopelessly, sitting with Robert Frost in the garden we'd rolled into, and listening to D.H. Lawrence and Frieda as they shouted and threw things at each other in her tiny kitchen. And sometimes she would read us some of their poetry. And hers.

Eleanor has been celebrated for her prose – memoirs, plays, revue sketches (with her brother Herbert) and her wonderful books for children. But her poetry, with the exception, of course, of 'Morning Has Broken' and 'Mrs Malone' with Edward Ardizzone's delicate and witty illustrations, has been neglected. Some of it may have dated and seem a bit whimsical or sentimental now, but there's such variety here, such playfulness and *joie de vivre*, and sometimes such depth so simply expressed.

Take, for example, in the section on Childhood, among the skipping and chanting poems and the games with names, the one called 'It Was Long Ago': a beautiful evocation of a remembered moment, particular and yet spilling light, as all good poems must, onto something wider. The way Eleanor gently buttonholes the reader, creating a conversational intimacy into which to place the last crucial line:

Then I grew up you see

Or how in 'The Reflection' she seems to tell her life story in 10 four line verses. It begins:

> She had no life except to be what men
> Required of her to be.
> They came again for sympathy, and came again
> For sympathy.

Edward Thomas, the love of her life, inspires some of her best verse and the poems dedicated to his memory carry a special charge. My favourite is the short 'Easter Monday' written in his memory after the news of his death in France in 1917, with its heartbreaking ending:

> There are three letters that you will not get.

I love the games with words. 'Books' ought to be pinned up in every threatened public library – and the poems in praise of cats (what *was* the one called curled up in the chair that first visit?) and as an ex-BBC man, I find the affectionate, sometimes slightly mocking tone with which she addresses that great institution in her 'ABC of the BBC', extremely refreshing:

> On Friday you shall hear a play
> On Saturday you'll dance so gay
> On Sunday there's a poet who
> Will come to read to me and you
> On Monday there's a humorist
> Who certainly must not be missed,
> On Tuesday there's a concert, and
> On Wednesday there's a famous Band,
> On Thursdays there's a special Star
> To talk to us—and there you are!

Gilbert and Sullivan meet Hilaire Belloc.

Eleanor is rightly famous for her children's writing and almost everything she does has that powerful mixture of mystery and repetition that children love. It is very evident in the charming selections from 'The Town Child's Alphabet' and 'The Nursery Rhymes of London Town', but, for me, it's when she reins in her gaiety and playfulness to touch something very deep in herself – lost love, remembered friendship, inevitable parting – that she writes her best poetry. 'We May Not Say We Love' is a perfect 12 line rhyming distillation of the difference between feeling and showing. It ends:

> *"I love" is what we must not say*
> *Even when we look it.*

while the poem dedicated to Denys Blakelock that begins:
"Do not be sad for a day that seems swiftly ended..." is one of the best poems about friendship I know.

When my wife, Poh Sim, and I got married on a beautiful September day in 1964, Eleanor, who had stood by us during a great deal of Montaguing and Capuleting, wasn't well enough to be there, but she presented us with signed copies of a dozen of her books. We went off to Africa after the wedding and never saw her again. But the books are still on the shelf and these poems bring her wonderfully back:

And while she hummed, and the cat purred, I remember
How she filled a saucer with berries and cream for me
So long ago,

Such berries and such cream as I remember
I never had seen before, and never see
Today you know.

And that is almost all I can remember,
The house, the mountain, the grey cat on her knee,
Her red shawl, and the tree,
And the taste of the berries, the feel of the sun I remember
And the smell of everything that used to be
So long ago...

Piers Plowright
Hampstead, May 2012

INTRODUCTION

"In my youth I dreamed of being a real poet but half-way through my life the dream died, and whatever figments of it remained went into writing songs and verses for children..." wrote Eleanor Farjeon in 1951, in the Foreword to her collection of poems *Silver-Sand and Snow*.

She under-rated herself, which is why, in this new selection over sixty years later, I want to take a closer look at the wide range and diversity of her writing, and introduce it to new readers.

It has become too easy to label her as the celebrated, prize-winning children's writer, or the cosy, bespectacled cat-loving woman once, surprisingly in love with Edward Thomas, or as the writer of the lyric *Morning Has Broken,* a hit record in the seventies. Working alongside her niece, Annabel Farjeon, researching for the biography of her aunt, I grew close to members of her family, and discovered the depth, passion and endearing personality of a quite unique woman. Perhaps I allowed myself to grow even closer when I portrayed her in a dramatised programme on the life of the poet Edward Thomas. Now, as her executor, dealing daily with requests for her poems for anthologies or for broadcasts, answering queries about her families on both sides of the Atlantic, giving permission for her character to be written into a novel or a play, both of these underway as I write, I feel both protective and increasingly in awe.

Her early poetry has been largely dismissed as over-romantic and derivative, and I admit that I turned back to it with some trepidation. I found that I was wrong, and that titles like *Pan Worship* (1908) and *Dream-Songs For The Beloved* (1911) deserved re-reading. Although these books, published in her twenties, tended to dwell on her unhappiness and sense of failure in both love and life, there were indications of a more discerning writer. It has been rewarding to re-read them, and to include some poems here.

It would have been good to have her opinion of this collection taken from so many different sources. I like to think that she would approve of choices gleaned from her early work, her sonnets to Edward Thomas, her more journalistic off-beat writing, and the poetry written with children in mind. She made clear in her 1941 essay *Magic Casements* (published by P.E.N.) her gratitude for the unwieldy lack of selection in her childhood reading. Her father's study *the little bookroom*, offered *much trash and more treasure. Riffraff and gentle-folk and noblemen, a lottery, a lucky dip.* Readers will discover an equally haphazard and somewhat unexpected choice here. The notes for each section aim to place the poems in context where possible and, although this is not a biography, to add background.

Eleanor Farjeon knew she wanted to be a writer from a very early age, and was given every encouragement by her writer father, Benjamin Leopold ("Ben") Farjeon.

B. L. Farjeon was born in London's East End in 1838, son of a Sephardi Jewish family who had emigrated, it is believed, from the Iberian Peninsula. A clever boy, circumstances forced him to leave school early and to work as a printer's devil on a newspaper. A good choice for a lover of words, and though the hours were long and the pay small, one bonus was being able to peer into the window of a second-hand book shop on the way to work. The bookseller observed him one day, through the window, greedily reading the open pages of Fouque's *Undine*. Next day he turned the pages for him, coming out to suggest: "You are fond of reading, my boy?" When Ben explained that there were few books in his home, the kindly man told him that the bookshop was to be his library.

Eleanor Farjeon loved that story, as she loved all the stories her parents told of their lives. They were good stories, colourful, varied, exciting; in Ben's case, almost the stuff of fairy tales. He was the poor boy given money by a better-off uncle to travel to Australia with thoughts of adventure and gold. No gold was found, but there was adventure in plenty. He took many tough outdoor jobs, living on a shoestring, and writing stories; some getting published in magazines. When he moved to New Zealand he secured a position on a newspaper, the Otago Daily Times, and worked his way up to becoming manager, then deputy editor of the paper.

As time went on, he began to move in artistic circles, meeting writers, musicians, actors. His lively personality, vitality and enthusiasm attracted him to people. He wrote his first novels. An actor who enjoyed his company was Joseph Jefferson, third in the theatrical dynasty of Jeffersons who in America rivalled England's Irvings and Terrys. By the 1870s Ben's books had become popular, turning out to be amongst the favourite reading of Jefferson's daughter, Margaret. She longed to meet this author, and when she did the two fell in love and married.

The story of their meeting is told by their daughter in her book *A Nursery in the Nineties*, which also relates the story of the childhood shared with her three brothers, Harry, Joe and Herbert.

Ben and Maggie's first child, Harry was born in Hohokus, New Jersey in 1878, and in 1879 they returned to London to apartments in Buckingham Street, just off the Strand. A second baby, Charley was born in 1880, a delicate child, who died when his sister Eleanor was a baby. Eleanor's birth on the 13th February 1881 was marked by her proud father with an announcement in the *London Figaro* followed by a prophecy in verse:

> *Imperious Babe! that yet can scarcely speak*
> *Doth rival Chanticleer with piercing shriek.*
> *May not those lungs which now such yells emit*
> *One day enthral a world with sense and wit.*

After the birth in 1883 of Joseph Jefferson (called after his actor grandfather), the family moved to Adelaide Road, Hampstead, in North London, settling in a bigger house at the end of the road when Herbert (Bertie) was born in 1887, the Golden Jubilee Year. The childhood years of the four Farjeons are brought to life vividly and in great detail in the memoir, fascinating to read in the light of today's changing ideas on education. Their mixed heritage undoubtedly benefited them.

Eleanor would say that her father was a Jew by instinct as well as race, but did not practice his religion…*"a devout believer without a creed…"* he passed on to his children a sense of tradition, generosity and an enduring work ethic. Their mother Maggie's Christian beliefs and love of music and entertainment inherited from her theatrical family mingled satisfyingly. The Farjeons' gatherings, especially Christmas parties master-minded by the exuberant Ben, were legendary. When Eleanor was 82, she recalled in a broadcast:

I and my brothers, Harry, Joe and Bertie, were born with books and the theatre in our blood. Our childhood received its tremendous imaginative stimulus from the actors and authors, painters and musicians who were our parents' friends. My father told our Nursery Governess to teach us nothing that we didn't want to learn. I read avidly with a mind that was never disciplined, never learnt how to know all of one thing while it gleaned smatterings of a thousand others. I grew up dreamily in a world of illusion that continued unbrokenly and dangerously until I was nearly thirty.

Perhaps that word *dangerously* reads oddly, but it was only in later years that she fully realised the true effect of the years of excessively imaginative play and ritual. Her brother Harry used his fertile imagination and inventive brain to create a compelling game in which he and Nellie (her family name) became, at his command, characters from books, plays, and fairy tales. All children play imaginatively; this game became *too* intense, and reached a degree of accomplishment from which, at times, it was hard to break away. Harry was in control, choosing the characters while she followed his wishes.

Guided by Harry's direction I played my part, emotionally absorbed. When I should have been growing up it was a harmful check on life itself for its imaginative extension did not include natural knowledge.

"I never had any trouble bringing you up," recalled their Mother, a pretty, gentle, delicate foil for her dark, exuberant, dynamic husband, "I left all that to Harry."

If their father appeared to dominate the home—*"How jolly he was! how sudden! how like the thunderstorms he loved to watch... this exciting, excitable... unreasonable... honourable... generous... irritable, father of ours!"* wrote Eleanor... it was Harry who dominated the Nursery. *His* word was Law and the Rules that he made must be kept. This extraordinary boy had a fertile imagination and brain, was a glutton for fairness and truth, and a stickler for order. He set "Bedtimes" for his siblings, and not until Eleanor was 16 did she defy him over her 9 pm curfew. There were Rules about touching each others books or toys, dipping biscuits into tea, putting things away, washing hands before touching his beloved piano.

There was also the *Rule of October 11th, 3 O'Clock. On that date and at that time each member of the Family shall take special note of what he or she is doing, and, if they are separated, shall tell each other*. This particular Rule was carried on into adult life.

Of course life wasn't all guided by Rules. Harry instigated wonderfully inventive games, indoors and out, Hoop Games, Marble Matches, Pencil and Paper Games, Competitions, a Sunday Fete, Garden Cricket, Boat sailing on the Whitestone Pond.

In *A Nursery in the Nineties* Eleanor Farjeon shows insight into the characters of her brothers, and describes herself quite openly, revealing the burden throughout her childhood of recurring headaches and sickness and nights of sleeplessness when she would lie awake, inventing stories. In the chapter *Nellie* she writes,

When I try to make a picture of myself it seems to me that I was a dreamy, timid, sickly, lachrymose, painfully shy, sensitive, greedy, ill-regulated little girl; not selfish on the whole, very affectionate and desirous of affection, almost as unwilling to inflict pain as to suffer it (I was a coward in most respects) and intensely absorbed in my writing, my reading, my family and my imaginative life.

She worshipped her Mother, seeing her as a beautiful romantic figure; one she could never match in grace, charm and elegance. Her memoir draws on the occasions when Maggie would appear in dress and adornments worn for a theatre outing or ball before tucking her daughter into bed. At children's parties she would cling to her. Early note-books included loving verses to "Mama"; she craved her advice and approval.

It was from Maggie that she inherited a closeness to her American heritage, showing great pride in her famous actor grandfather. From her mother she was well versed in American theatre history. In 1938 she would be asked to write the Foreword to *The Unlocked Book,* the story of the actor, John Wilkes Booth, now mainly remembered for the assassination of the President, Abraham Lincoln.

By the time he had a family, Ben Farjeon was well known in the literary world, much influenced by his passion for Dickens. He had a library of 8,000 books where his children were invited to browse. On Sundays each child was given a book to keep. Eleanor's first was Tennyson's *In Memoriam.* The late Eileen Colwall, writer and librarian, wrote in *The Bodley Head Monograph* on Eleanor Farjeon:

She was fed on poetry...Elizabethan lyrics, Shakespeare, Keats and Shelley...her father never made her read any particular book, but when he read to her from a new author he had "wound up the watch and it went of itself." Her favourites were Dumas, the Grecian romances, innumerable fairy tales and "the Greeks," her lifelong friends...Writing was an essential part of life to all the Farjeons. Ben Farjeon wrote endlessly and used the first Remington typewriter ever seen in England. He taught his young daughter of seven how to type, to correct proofs and to read copy.

It was little wonder that the eye specialist, prescribing spectacles for the short sighted Harry and Nellie, and offering advice about reading clear print in a good light, was amazed to be shown the eight year old girl's copy of Sir Philip Sidney's *Arcadia* for his approval.

Poems and stories penned by Ben's children were carefully copied and treasured in special notebooks. In the years 1889 and 1890, when Eleanor was aged 8 and 9, she appears to have been especially prolific. The notebook includes 29 poems on subjects of *Nature, Spring, Animals* and especially *Love* as in a fervent poem addressed to her 'sweetheart', Button, one of the sons of their close friends, the nearby, theatrical Albery family.

> *My heart has never beat before*
> *As it did beat just now,*
> *I want you but to keep to me*
> *And I'll give my hand to thou.*
>
> *I'll never turn away from thee*
> *If always you keep true,*
> *But if you always turn away*
> *I will not keep to you.*
>
> *You've turned away from me just once*
> *But if you won't again*
> *I'll give you all the love my heart*
> *Will ever and can contain.*

This is signed: *Nellie Farjeon March 3rd 1889, Bournemouth, a fortnight after her 8th birthday*.

Looking ahead thirty years to the time when she wrote topical verse for newspapers and journals it is interesting to find she was writing, aged 9 –

THE FIVE ADVERTISEMENTS OF HAPPINESS

1.

I write you down a very long list through and through
Of things you ought to have and things you ought to do,
You'll always be happy and always have hope
So long as you wash with "PEARS PATENT SOAP."

2

Of course you like the things that are very nice to eat,
And there is one thing that in your house ought to have a seat.
Some people say it isn't good but then they're very fellish
For you couldn't get along without
                              "GOODALL'S YORKSHIRE RELISH."

3.
I think you like the things that are the very best
And I don't think that you will get any rest
If you don't eat the things that for you are good
So it's always best to keep a quantity of "NESTLE'S FOOD."

(Two more verses and then, to close):
6.
But oh! there's something else that I ought to have said before,
And of this more than the others you ought to have a store.
It'll cure you of your pains and cure you of your ills
So always keep a box of "BEECHAM'S PATENT PILLS."

Nellie Farjeon, April 9th 1890, London

She showed her father everything she wrote, and then ran away with a stomach-ache and lay down until he came to tell her what he thought.

I almost always agreed with his corrections…but once we had a tussle about a word. I had been reading some antique romances, and liked the queer language they were written in: therefore in my own ALAN-A-DALE I wrote,

> *O gentle is my own true–love*
> *And like a flower is she,*
> *But they have riven her mefrom*
> *A rich man's wife to be…*

Papa scratched out the "me" and put it after the "from".
*"I don't mean that" I said. I meant "mefrom". "Why?" asked Papa. "Because it's an **old** way of saying it."*

Then Papa became very emphatic about "from me" being better than "mefrom" because it was more natural and he did not want me to write affectedly. When Papa had gone out I changed it back and never let him see it.

Despite the later success of her writing in prose, poetry, drama and song, in the early days she allowed *romance* to take over and was always suspicious of editorial intervention.

On another occasion Ben Farjeon was excited by his daughter's epic poem *Chaos*...sixty lines of formally structured blank verse, closing with:

And when at eventide we're thinking o'er
The sorrows or the pleasures of the day
'Tis Chaos we must thank for this fair life.
And thus continue all those worlds of his
In animation, health and wealth and joy,
Tasting the fruitful pleasures of the earth
Whose cultivation keeps us now alive.
But not for ever. Then will come the cry
"Chaos is dead!" and all will be destroyed
That he has done. But now, and until then,
We'll live in peace, and love, and happiness.

Little wonder that he hurried to his Club with the copy, confident that no other member had an 11 year old daughter capable of such a masterpiece.

"I have hopes of you, Nell, I have hopes of you" he said, after reading a short story she had shown him..."*It is the best thing you have written. I think you're going to make a writer."* She would carry these words with her through the troubled times to come.

Eleanor loved her brothers and their home life together... the nursery slogan *"We're Harry – Nellie – Joe –and Bertie! We are us!"* was warm and comforting, but outside the family she was shy and gauche, feeling unattractive in her spectacles, and missing all that had been familiar and safe.

There was inevitable change. Harry, a brilliant pianist from early childhood, became the youngest student at the

Royal Academy of Music. Joe and Bertie, more worldly than their elders, were off on their own pursuits, frequently haunting Lords' Cricket Ground, or huddled over their own creation, a family magazine. *Farjeon's Weekly* was launched with contributions from Harry and Nellie; but the pressure of frequent publishing forced the young editors to re-think, and *Farjeon's Fortnightly* proved more manageable. These two, who were given some outside schooling, were born editors, and in their adult careers, as writers, reaped the benefits of their Nursery exploits.

After her father's death in 1903, followed by changes in the family's circumstances, Ben had been over generous and unpredictable all of his gregarious outgoing life, life seemed dark. A highlight for her was being invited by Harry to write the libretti for two of his operettas. These were well received by critics and audiences and her contribution much praised with due attention given to her youth: she was eighteen.

Although some early stories were published in magazines, two years after her father's death she wrote, in an unpublished memoir,

I see myself at the age of 24 in retreat in my little top room trying to sublimate in pen and ink the unripe emotions of my fantasy life. I sat for nine tenths of the time with my pen in my idle hand. The fault lay in me, in my idle procrastinating, greedy, self-indulgent, undisciplined nature. Every day I spent hours shut up in my room hoping to delude the household into a belief that "Nellie was working!"

Between the years of 1905 and 1911 life opened up considerably as she found a direction for her writing.

In 1908 the respected publisher Elkin Matthews published a small collection, *Pan Worship*. Later, wanting to forget the days when she wrote of trees as *"Temples of Pan"* she told a friend *"I don't look at it now… I'm afraid it's rather bad!"*

There are, though, moments worth re-capturing, like these lines describing a lark:

No other bird flies up so high
And shakes its sparkling spray of song
Through the grey clouds in the sky.
No other bird has just that thrilling
Note in trilling,
Or can sustain so long
Its liquid flood of mirth:
As rare a book as God's dew is to earth.
Yet it is afternoon.
I thought the larks, all scorning
The jaded hours, sang only in the morning...

This was 1908, a few years before Edward Thomas would add to her knowledge of wildlife.

Professor Judy Kendall, researching for *Edward Thomas's Poets* (Carcanet 2012) was discerning in relating Farjeon's 1911 poem *Poplars At Night* (included here in the section *The Gate In The Wall*) to Thomas's *Aspens* (1915), one of his most admired poems. Her friend, Clifford Bax, published the poem in her 1911 book, with its rather fanciful title *Dream Songs For The Beloved,* in a series linked to his magazine of mystical art, *Orpheus.*

She had perfected a facility to adopt the tone and style of earlier poets, a gift she drew on later when writing for theatre, and in 1910 her invention of a supposedly long-forgotten Elizabethan poet, Nathaniel Downes, formed a curious story. She feigned a 16th Century style filling the tale with lyrics as if written by *Natty Downes* to his beloved, *Annys...*

When I smell th'enchaunted muske
Of awak'ning flowers at duske
    I doe thinke upon hir.
Or when litil riuers leape
Tinkling downe an emerald steepe
Where th'enamelled florets peepe,
    Then I thynke upon hir...

Published in 1911 in Blackwood's Magazine, it foiled some literary critics, who were excited by the discovery of this unknown poet, but the Poet Laureate, Robert Bridges was less convinced, and when Edward Thomas read her "hoax" he was sceptical.

Although this facet of her writing, along with the mastery of "punning", innuendo, and word-play would become known through her *Tomfool* column in the Daily Herald few will have seen the rather charming Victorian pieces, in the vein of *vers de societe* published in John Hadfield's *The Saturday Book for 1964*, the year before her death. A verse from one called *Sister Mine* catches the period style:

> He is waiting over there,
>   Sister mine
> With a very pensive air,
>   Sister mine,
> He settles and unsettles
>   His cravat,
> He is counting daisy-petals—
>   Think of that!
> When I passed he turned his head
>   Growing very very red,
> And he said — but what he said
>   I divine,
> Was for **your** ear, not for mine,
>   Sister mine!

Back in 1911 she was emerging from her shell of unease and shyness. With Harry more involved at the Academy, and Joe marrying early, she and her youngest brother, Bertie, grew closer together. They became part of a lively, interesting group of young people, who, she wrote '*caused some uneasiness by our advanced ideas on Socialism, Art, the Woman's Vote and Sex*'. Amongst the friends were musicians like Myra Hess, Harriet Cohen, Arnold Bax; Arnold's brother Clifford, and young doctors Maitland Radford and Godwin Baynes. Often with them were pianist Gertrude Peppercorn and her husband the versatile writer, performer and artist Stacy Aumonier, the sisters Joan and Rosalind Thornycroft. Others came and went, different lively young circles intermingling for theatre visits, tennis parties, gatherings that included inventing games and entertainments. The time before the Great War was often remembered for the visit of the Ballet Russe, and the magic created by Diaghilev, Nijinsky and Karsavina.

By 1912, her brother Bertie had met Edward Thomas, at that time undergoing treatment for his depressive illness by Godwin Baynes, a disciple of Jung. Edward Thomas suggested that Bertie brought Eleanor, along with Rosalind Thornycroft, for tea in the Strand's Cottage Tea-Rooms. She was at once attracted to the writer, whom she knew was married with three children, and overburdened and wearied with the pressure of reviewing, and writing commissions for articles and books.

Their friendship and her love for him have been included in every book about him, and not always with understanding of her character, behaviour and feelings. Her own memoir *Edward Thomas: The Last Four Years* remains the most insightful. She does not hide her feelings for him, but using his actual letters to her – over 200 in four years – gives her the opportunity to link them to her own thoughts as well as to the events and people in her life.

She said herself that she loved once, more than she would ever love in the same way again. Edward Thomas, despite his shifting moods and irritability, the unhappiness he caused his family, the knowledge that this was an unrequited love, became essential to her being.

I am frequently asked about her contribution to his life. It is known that she typed his poetry for him when he first wrote it, and assisted with sending it to publishers; in short she became his literary confidante and trusted amanuensis, but few have acknowledged her in the same vein as his other friends, Gordon Bottomley or Robert Frost.

I think that her friendship was necessary to him. It is always flattering to know that someone loves you, it is encouraging if your family likes that person, so that maybe the mood lightens too, pleasing everyone. It also helps to have a friend who knows the publishing world, is astute and keen, and, most importantly, believes in your work. The letters give an indication of how much he relied on her, constantly asked her advice, requested help, suggested meeting for tea or a meal or a walk, and invited her down to his home in Steep. In short, he valued this friendship.

Although this is an all too familiar quotation I repeat it here: the morning after Eleanor Farjeon had read his essays in *Light & Twilight*, she asked him, *shyly, and rather inadequately:*

"*Haven't you ever written poetry, Edward?*"

His well known reply came: "*Me? I couldn't write a poem to save my life*".

This was a few days after his first meeting with Robert Frost, and in the summer of 1914 she was privileged to walk with the two poets, while they shared *an endless duologue on the nature of poetry.*

I have wondered how much of that discussion on speech, poetry, and the cadences of the human voice was absorbed by her. Certainly a change in her writing came towards the end of the First World War as is shown in the Sonnets. The closing *Second Love* sonnets have a freshness and immediacy, lacking some of the self-consciousness in her earlier ones.

For an emotional woman, deeply caring of people, she had an unexpected reaction to Death. "*Death is not the greatest heartbreak,*" she once wrote "*Life gives us much harder things to bear than the deaths of those who love us, whom we love.*" When Edward Thomas died, those four years remained in her memory as a crucial part of her life.

He had enjoyed and approved of her first popular book in 1916, *Nursery Rhymes of London Town*, which arose from the verses she had published in the magazine *Punch*. It was followed in 1917 by *More Nursery Rhymes*, equally enjoyed by Victor Haslam, a young soldier with whom she had become friends through correspondence. It was to Haslam she sent chapters of her next book *Martin Pippin in the Apple Orchard,* a collection of linked stories as told by a wandering minstrel. She wrote these while living in Houghton, Sussex, in a rented cowman's cottage, declaring in an unpublished memoir that she was alone and independent for the first time in thirty-six years, and felt it to be an important turning point in her life. Sussex became from then onwards, a second home. *Martin Pippin,* published in 1920, was an instant success going into several reprints. It was dedicated to Victor Haslam and after meeting him it seemed they might share a future together. It was not to be and the ending of the relationship caused much distress. Around this time she was working for P.E.N. the organisation involved with helping writers, artists and musicians internationally. Her thoughts on war, its rights and wrongs, are revealed in sonnets and articles of this period.

After the war her writing career moved quickly as confidence and belief in herself grew. All she had read from early childhood onward, all the imaginative ideas, stories, legends, classics and folk-tales informed her writing. Like her father, a great story-teller, she invented endearing characters, and wove wonderfully crafted stories. She was also, as one tends to forget, a gifted composer – not in the same class as her brother, Harry – but with no formal teaching and a fine ear for rhythm she set many of her own poems to music, and was also asked to set the words of other writers. Her settings for *Nursery Rhymes of London Town* were, in the 1930s and 1940s sung in primary schools, and later her settings for *Kings & Queens* show her skill at relating words to music. Like the poems of her friend Walter de la Mare, her songs and verses for children cross barriers finding unexpected readers of all ages who respond to them.

By her phrase *"a real poet"* quoted at the start of this introduction, she was thinking of Wordsworth, Shelley or Keats, all of whom inspired her early response to poetry, and when she was nearly forty she decided to share her life with a true lover of these poets, George Chester Earle. Known as "Pod" he was an inspired teacher of English, who during the war had briefly met Edward Thomas with her. She cherished the one conversation heard between the two men, feeling they had like minds. Earle was separated from his wife. *"We formed,"* she wrote, *"as true a bond of marriage as could be without benefit of clergy."* They lived in Eleanor's cottage in Hampstead and a cottage in Sussex, with some disapproval from her mother Maggie, but those friends and family who visited the couple found, in the words of dancer Yoma Sasburgh, *a place away from the world.* Keats was frequently quoted, there was always a kettle filled with boiling water for cups of tea; wonderful conversations, stories, and many cats.

By the end of the 1920s all four Farjeons were successful in their careers. Harry was a much loved teacher at the Royal Academy, students amused and intrigued by his eccentricities. As his sight grew worse he wore an eye shade permanently against the light. One ex-student, Steve Race, told me how much he thanked Harry for his own musical success, and would never forget him.

Joe Jefferson Farjeon moved to Sussex with his American wife, Frances Wood, and their daughter Joan. He was a most prolific writer, his adventure stories and witty journalism captured devoted fans, and his detective stories became Crime Club favourites. One book *Number 17*, a best-seller, he made into a play which was produced in the West End, and the story-line was used by Alfred Hitchcock for the screen play of a film of the same name.

Herbert – Bertie – Farjeon had the most diverse career of all. His tongue-in cheek journalism for various papers was found hugely readable, and alongside this he became one of the leading theatre critics of his time. His knowledge of Shakespeare from childhood magnified, and he edited the annotated *Shakespeare* volumes for the Nonsuch Press, and presented programmes on Shakespearian characters for the BBC. Alongside all this he wrote sophisticated, satirical revues for the London theatre, his sister occasionally supplying ideas. Many stars of the period took part; one of his discoveries being Joyce Grenfell, performing at a party before she became a star entertainer.

Around 1930 Eleanor and Herbert Farjeon began working on a book about the Monarchy, and created the motto for their shared work *"Collaborators' Honour"*. It was to remain a secret who wrote which lines. Published in 1932 the poems, with their range of verse patterns and witty takes on the Kings and Queens from William I to our Queen Elizabeth II, were immediate best sellers and have remained popular.

They followed this with a similar collection based on the heroes and heroines they had learnt about in childhood, and then embarked on some ideas for theatre musicals. For Eleanor Farjeon this involvement with theatre, as well as the sharing of writing with one of her brothers, added to her growing confidence, and gave another dimension to the writing for children, for which she was best known. Readers of her many books for the young knew nothing of the range of her work; the poems that appeared in Socialist papers under pseudonyms, or the hymns included in the second edition of *Songs of Praise* in 1931. One of these hymns, *"Morning Has Broken"* would become famous after her death, and for some is almost synonymous with her name.

On the subject of *Writing for Children* she was decisive, as an article for *The Writers' Desk Book* (1934) shows. Amongst useful and practical advice comes this: *'Write only what **you** will enjoy writing…Don't "write down" to children; don't try to be on their level (you were once but forgot it when you left it); don't think there is a special way of addressing children which they will cotton to, a special tone of voice they will respond to. There may be – but don't **you** go looking for it!'*

And she closes with the example of *a certain teacher* after whose Poetry class a small boy of 9, enchanted and uncomprehending, ran round the playground, waving his arms, shouting again and again, *"There **was** a time! There **was** a time! There **was** a time!"*

Those who knew him, their many friends, would instantly recognise Pod as that teacher who had taught Wordsworth to his young pupils at King Alfred's School, Hampstead.

She was to outlive Pod and her brothers. Herbert Farjeon died, following a fall, in 1945, before their fairy-tale extravaganza, *The Glass Slipper* was to have its second Christmas run at London's St. James's Theatre. Harry died in 1948, Pod in 1949 and Joe in 1955.

In her *'latter years'*, as she called them, much of her time was spent in recalling the past. The most important work was in sorting through her letters from Edward Thomas and linking them with her own memories of the four years of their friendship. Her health was often poor, and her eye-sight growing worse, and there are the occasional errors over dating a letter, if Thomas had not included one.

However the book *Edward Thomas: The Last Four Years* came out to great acclaim and excellent reviews in 1958, a welcome addition to the growing body of work about the poet who had been most neglected amongst the poets of the First World War.

Amongst the many writers who were friends, her nieces and nephew and their families, she had one particular friend, Denys Blakelock. Some twenty years her junior, they struck up a warm and loving friendship in 1949, which until her death, filled the gap left by Pod and her brothers. A fine actor, and himself a writer, they shared many theatre and literary friends, and his memoir *Eleanor: Portrait of a Farjeon* is a personal reminder of that time. It was during this friendship that she took instruction from a priest and was received into the Catholic Church of St James, Spanish Place, London, at the age of seventy. For much of her life she had felt the need of a more formal spiritual guidance, and this decision brought her much joy.

Although she was rather shy, with her friend Walter de la Mare she occasionally gave readings of her poems in a school in the East End, and broadcast the talk on her childhood for the BBC, mentioned earlier. It was following the publication of her collection of stories *The Little Bookroom* in 1955 that she won three awards, the Hans Andersen Award, the Carnegie Medal, and the Regina Medal of the American Catholic Library Association, but she turned down the offer to be made a Dame of the British Empire, explaining that she did not want to be different from the milkman.

The editing of selections of Frost's and Thomas's poems for young readers were important tasks; writing of the two poets brought back memories of the two weeks' holiday in 1914 spent with them, their families and the group who would later be known as the Dymock Poets. Robert Frost, visiting England in 1957 to receive various University honours, made a point of spending time with her in Hampstead, talking of the past as well as their current work.

Her health was failing when writing the introduction to the Edward Thomas selection, *The Green Roads*. She wrote in bed and several drafts were attempted and discarded. Writing to a friend she said: "*I hope I shall do it well enough, though of course I won't. When does one ever?...*"

It was typed eleven times before she felt satisfied, and the completed manuscript was posted on 12th February 1965. She never saw it in print. She died on 5 June 1965, and is buried in the little churchyard close to St Mary's, Holly Hill, in Hampstead.

In 1981 I wrote a radio programme for her centenary, and interviewed several people who had known and loved her. "*She was the best friend of every friend she had,*" Grace Hogarth, who had been her editor, told me. "*No one was ever turned away.*" She might appear rather cuddly and comfortable as she aged, but those who really knew her found a tougher personality. She did not suffer fools gladly, was astute in her handling of anyone who cheated her, or used her expertise and then let her down.

Almost 50 years after her death not a week goes by without something happening to do with her... a request for a story or poem for an anthology or a broadcast, a query about her work for P.E.N., the poems she wrote under pseudonyms – *Tomfool* for the *Daily Herald*, *Merry Andrew* for the *Labour Leader*, *Chimaera* for *Time & Tide* – and there are always new students and researchers with questions about her friendship with Edward Thomas.

When Ben Farjeon prophesied that his daughter might *one day enthral a world with sense and wit* he little guessed that he was very near the truth. The Society of Children's Publishers, known as the *Children's Book Circle* gives an annual prize, *The Eleanor Farjeon Award,* to someone who has offered an outstanding contribution to the Literature for young readers, a fitting memory of the child who first discovered Stories and Poetry in the eighteen-nineties, in the little bookroom.

Anne Harvey, July 2012

Like Sorrow Or A Tune

CHILDHOOD'S FLICKERING SHADOW

GOOD MORNING

    Good-morning now.
Wake body,
Wake mind!
Work, play,
Seek, find.
Eat breakfast,
Dinner too,
Wake, brush,
Sing, dance, and do!
    Good-morning now!

WAKING UP

Oh! I have just had such a lovely dream!
And then I woke,
And all the dream went out like kettle-steam,
Or chimney-smoke.

My dream was all about—how funny, though!
I've only just
Dreamed it, and now it has begun to blow
Away like dust.

In it I went—no! in my dream I had —
No, that's not it!
I can't remember, oh, it is *too* bad,
My dream a bit.

But I saw something beautiful I'm sure —
Then someone spoke,
And then I didn't see it any more,
Because I woke.

THERE ISN'T TIME!

There isn't time, there isn't time
To do the things I want to do,
With all the mountain-tops to climb
And all the woods to wander through,
And all the seas to sail upon,
And everywhere there is to go,
And all the people, every one
Who lives upon the earth to know.
There's only time, there's only time
To know a few, and do a few,
And then sit down and make a rhyme
About the rest I want to do.

THE OLD MAN'S TOES

Up the street,
Down the street,
My
    Joan
         goes —
(Mind you don't tread
      upon the
Old
    Man's
          Toes!)
She hops along the
      pavement
Into every Square,
But she mustn't touch
      the   Cracks   in
        between
Them
        There.
The Squares on the pavement
Are safe

        as can be:
One is the Sands
By the side
            of the
                    sea;
One is a Garden where
Joan's
      flowers
                grow,
One is a Meadow
She
      and I
            know,
But the Cracks are   *dangerous,*
As
      Everybody
                  knows!

The Cracks in the Pavement are the
Old
      Man's
            Toes.
Any one who treads on the
Old
      Man's
            Corn
Will wish in a jiffy he had
Never
      been
            born!
For the Sea will roll up and
Suck
      you
            down!
And a horrid blight will turn your
Garden
            brown!

5

And into the Meadow with an
Angry
  Moo
A Big Cross Cow will come
Rushing
   at
    You!
Up the street and down the street
My
 Joan
   goes —
Here she makes a   Pudding,
There she smells a Rose,
Yonder she goes stooping where the
Mushroom
   grows—
(Mind, Joan! don't tread upon the
Old
 Man's
   Toes!)

BRAVERY

The cow in the meadow
 Looks sideways at me —
 But what do I care?
 With my chin in the air,
I stare at the stile,
 Or a cloud, or a tree,
When the cow in the meadow
 Looks sideways at me.

The cow in the meadow
 Is not more than three
 And you're not very bold
 When you're not very old,
So I mustn't alarm her—

6

She's *timid,* you see,
And that's why she always
    Looks sideways at me.

She gives me my milk
    And my butter for tea.
    'Git on!' says John,
    And at once she gits on —
And I stick to the footpath
    As brave as can be,
When the cow in the meadow
    Looks sideways at me.

HOUSE COMING DOWN

They're pulling down the house
    At the corner of the Square,
The floors and the ceilings
    Are out in the air,
The fireplaces so rusty,
The staircases so dusty
And wallpaper so musty
    Are all laid bare.

It looks like a dolls' house
    With the dolls put away,
And the furniture laid by
    Against another day;
No bed to lie in,
No pan to fry in,
Or dish to make a pie in,
    And nobody to play.

That was the parlour,
    With the cream-and-yellow scrawls,
That was the bedroom
    With the roses on the walls,

7

There's a dark red lining
 In the room they had for dining,
And a brown one, rather shining,
   Goes all up the halls.

But where is the lady
   In a pretty gown?
Where is the baby
   That used to crow and frown?
Oh, the room looks so little,
The house looks so brittle,
And no–one cares a tittle
   If it all tumbles down.

BLIND ALLEY

There's a turning I must pass
Often four times in a day,
Narrow, rather dark, with grass
Growing a neglected way;

Two long walls, a tumbled shed,
Rushes shadowing each wall —
When I've wondered where it led
People say, Nowhere at all.

But if that is true, oh why
Should this turning be at all?
Some time, in the daylight, I
Will creep up along the wall;

For it somehow makes you think,
It has such a secret air,
It might lead you to the brink
Of—oh well, of anywhere!

8

Some time I will go. And see,
Here's the turning just in sight,
Full of shadows beckoning me!
Some time, yes. But not to-night.

GIRLS' NAMES

What lovely names for girls there are!
There's Stella like the Evening Star,
And Sylvia like a rustling tree,
And Lola like a melody,
And Flora like a flowery morn,
And Sheila like a field of corn,
And Melusina like the moan
Of water. And there's Joan like Joan.

JOAN'S CORNER

Joan has a corner in a garden,
    The garden I am fondest of,
And of all the corners in the garden
    Hers is the one I love.

I'd rather play in Joan's Corner
    Than in the golden nurseries
Where Princes and Princesses sit
    And never make mud pies.

MEETING MARY

Hard by the Wildbrooks I met Mary,
Where berries smelled sweet and hot.
Mary, I fancy, was seven years old,
And I am never mind what.

"What are you getting?" I asked Mary.
"Blackberries. What are you?"
"Toadflax" I answered Mary, "and mushrooms."
"How many mushrooms?" "Two."

"Going to have blackberries stewed for dinner,
 Or blackberry jam?" said I.
"Not goin' to have neither." said Mary;
"Goin' to have blackberry pie."

"Aren't you lucky!" I said to Mary.
"And what sort of name have you got?"
"*My* name's Mary" said Mary. "What's your name?"
 I told her never mind what.

"Goodbye, Mary". "Goodbye" said Mary,
And went on picking and eating.
That's all about my meeting with Mary —
It's my favourite sort of meeting.

BRONWEN OF THE FLOWERS

Bronwen gathered wild flowers
Up-and-down the lane;
Her gathering touch upon them
Sweeter was than rain.

Now a blossom overblown,
Now a bud begun —
Her eye that lightened on them
Was quicker than the sun.

One by one she named them,
Oh, she did express
In her pretty namings
All their prettiness:

10

Some were fit for maidens,
Some for merry dames,
And the love with which she named them
Was lovelier than their names.

MYFANWY AMONG THE LEAVES

Dying leaf and dead leaf,
Yellow leaf and red leaf
And white-backed-beam
Lay along the woodland road
As quiet as a dream.

Summer was over,
The year had lost her lover,
Spent with her grief
All along the woodland road
Leaf fell on leaf.

Then came a shuffling,
Such a happy rustling
Of the dried sweet
Surf of leaves upon the road
Round a baby's feet.

Year-old leaf ran after
Three-year old laughter,
Danced through the air
As she caught them from the road
And flung them anywhere.

Old leaf and cold leaf,
Brown leaf and gold leaf
And white backed beam,
Followed down the woodland road
Myfanwy in a dream.

FOR JOAN

I have loved no other child,
Joan, as I love you;
The second life our children build
Remains for you to do.

You would have been out-loved in one
That never will be born,
And the love that should my flower have grown
Grows nothing but my thorn.

You for that unborn other's sake
My deepest heart do clutch,
But sometimes—sometimes all you take
Hurts, for her sake, too much.

GRISELDA

Griselda is greedy, I'm sorry to say.
She isn't contented with four meals a day,
Like breakfast and dinner and supper and tea
(I've had to put tea after supper—you see
             Why don't you?)
Griselda is greedy, as greedy can be.

    She snoops about the larder
    For sundry small supplies,
    She breaks the little crusty bits
    Of rims of apple pies,
    She pokes the roast-potato dish
    When Sunday dinner's done,
    And if there are two left in it
    Griselda snitches one.

Cold chicken and cold cauliflower
    She pulls in little chunks
    And when Cook calls
          "What *are* you doing there?"
            Griselda bunks.

Griselda is greedy. Well, that's how she feels,
She simply can't help eating in-between meals,
And always forgets what it's leading to, though
The Doctor has frequently told her: "You know
    Why, don't you?"
When the stomach-ache starts and Griselda says:
    "Oh!"

    She slips down to the dining-room
    When everyone's in bed,
    For cheese-rind on the supper-tray
    And buttered crusts of bread,
    A biscuit from the biscuit-box,
    Lump sugar from the bowl,
    A gherkin from the pickle-jar,
    Are all Griselda's toll;
    She tastes the salted almonds,
    And she tries the candied fruits—
And when Dad shouts:
          "Who *is* it down below?"
            Griselda scoots.

Griselda is greedy. Her relatives scold
And tell her how sorry she'll be when she's old,
She will lose her complexion, she's sure to grow fat,
She will spoil her inside—does she know what she's at?—
            (Why *do* they?)
Some people *are* greedy. Leave it at that.

HIDE-AND-SEEK (Hiding)

Tiptoe away! tiptoe away!
  While Jane is counting a hundred!
Where shall we go, above or below,
  While Jane is counting a Hundred?
      Under the table?
        No, Mabel
          is there!
Behind the wings of the grandfather chair!
  Hide in the curtain?
    I'm certain
      She'll see—
Creep away, creep away stealthily!

The linen-cupboard is warm and snug—
Peter's wrapped up in the travelling rug.
Don't whisper! don't giggle! *st !* look alive—
I'm sure she's got to Forty-five!
Under the bed is a lovely place—
Oh bother, it's full of Gwen and Grace—
The wardrobe is stuffed with Dick and Kate—
I'm certain she's got to Sixty-eight!
Up to the attics do a bunk,
Perhaps there's room in the wooden trunk—
No, it is crammed with Caroline,
She *must* have got to Seventy-nine!

Hide here! hide there! hide anywhere,
    While Jane is counting a Hundred!
        Be quick! be quiet! oh, do play fair
    While Jane is counting a Hundred!
          Hold your breath!
          Stand still as death!
Squeeze up, Roger, make room for Beth!
        Don't push!
              don't rush!
      She is coming—hush!
  She has finished counting her Hundred!

14

HIDE-AND-SEEK (Seeking)

When little Jane lifts up her head
     Uncovering her eyes,
Every other child has fled
     Into the mysteries,
The playmates that she knew are gone
     And Jane is left alone.

Oh Alice with the starry looks,
     Oh Ann with gleaming curls,
What dusky corners, what dim nooks
     Have hid you little girls?
The house is vast and Jane is small,
     And are you here at all?

Oh, Richard with the flashing smile,
     Oh Rob with freckled brow,
Where are you hiding all this while,
     You who were here but now?
The house lies in a sleep as deep
     As Sleeping Beauty's sleep.

Through all the rooms grown deaf and blind
     Jane seeks with throbbing heart
The hidden playmate whom to find
     Will make small tremors start—
For when she finds them in the game
     They may not be the same.

THE OTHER CHILD

When I put her in the swing
And set it going while I sing,
And all the apple-leaves of June
Shake in keeping with my tune,

And she cries merrily, sweet and shrill,
'Higher, higher, higher still!'—
Seated on an apple limb,
Invisible as air,
Watching this child bird-like skim
The speckled world of shade and sun,
Another child is there.

And every time my song is done,
This one, with her innocent brow
And blue eyes almost clear of fun,
Says, It is her turn now!
Lift me down and put her in,
And *I'll* sit on the apple-tree —
And then once over I begin
My song to sing
And rock the swing,
Where only I and this child see
Flying through the speckled air
The other child who's always there.

HERE WE GO ROUND THE MULBERRY BUSH

There is a bush that no-one sees,
The loveliest of little trees,
Full of sweet dark mulberries.

Round and round it children go,
Sometimes quick and sometimes slow,
Singing words all children know.

While they sing the bush is there
Planted in the empty air,
With fruit for every child to share.

Little girls with sandalled foot,
Little boys in clumping boot,
Running round the mulberry root,

Fair and dark ones, loitering, leaping,
Gay and grave ones, laughing, weeping,
Playing, working, waking, sleeping.

When the moment's game is done,
When the playing child is gone,
The unseen mulberry bush stands on,

And with all its leafy eyes
Childhood's flickering shadow spies
Dancing down the centuries,

And with all its leafy ears
Evermore the footstep hears
Of vanished childhood's hundred years,

Singing still without a sound,
Running silently around
The bush that never grew in ground.

BOYS' NAMES

What splendid names for boys there are!
There's Carol like a rolling car,
And Martin like a flying bird,
And Adam like the Lord's First Word,
And Raymond like the Harvest Moon
And Peter like a piper's tune
And Alan like the flowing on
Of water. And there's John, like John.

IN GOES ROBIN

In goes Robin, bold as brass,
Into all that moving mass
Of blue and green and creamy foam
Just as though he were at home.
Water doesn't frighten him,
He will sink till he can swim,
When a big wave knocks him down
Up will come his laughing brown
Spluttering face. He has no fear,
The sea is his: yes, all that clear
Stretch of water, touching all
The shores of earth, that makes its call
On English cliffs and Indian sands,
And coral-isles and mountain-lands,
And crowded ports and lonely bays:
His, should he choose to go those ways,
With all the ships that sail on it,
And all the gulls and mews that flit,
And all the fishes in the blue,
And all the wrecks and icebergs too.
The sea was Robin's from the first,
He saw it and was all athirst,
He couldn't wait to reach it—whether
Its waves were tumbled all together,
Or it was bright and smooth as glass,
In went Robin as bold as brass.

NED

It's a singular thing that Ned
Can't be got out of bed.
          When the sun comes round
          He is sleeping sound
With the blankets over his head.
          They tell him to shunt

And he gives a grunt,
And burrows a little deeper—
    He's a trial to them
    At eight a.m.
When Ned is a non-stop sleeper.
    Oh, the snuggly bits
    Where the pillow fits
    Into his cheek and neck!
    Oh, the beautiful heat
    Stored under the sheet
Which the breakfast bell will wreck!
Oo, the snoozly-oozly feel
He feels from head to heel,
    When to get out of bed
    Is worse to Ned
Than missing his morning meal!
                    But
It's a singular thing that Ned
After the sun is dead
    And the moon come round,
    Is not to be found,
And can't be got *into* bed!

BEDTIME

Five minutes, five minutes more, please!
    Let me stay five minutes more!
Can't I just finish the castle
    I'm building here on the floor?
Can't I just finish the story
    I'm reading here in my book?
Can't I just finish this bead-chain
    It *almost* is finished, look!
Can't I just finish this game, please!
    When a game's once begun
It's a pity never to find out
    Whether you've lost or won.

19

Can't I just stay five minutes?
        Well, can't I stay just four?
Three minutes, then? two minutes?
        Can't I stay *one* minute more?

GOOD NIGHT

        Now good-night!
Fold up your clothes
As you were taught,
Fold your two hands,
Fold up your thought;
Day is the plough-land,
Night is the stream,
Day is for doing,
Night is for dream.
        Now good-night.

A DRINK OF WATER

Mother has gone away. The night is black.
Whatever can I do to bring her back?
She tucked me in and kissed me once for all
And said good-night and told me not to call,
But oh, I want her so, I want her so!
What can I do to make her come? I know—
Mother! Mother! *Mo*-ther! (Listen! she's
Coming!) I want a drink of water, please.

Will she, when she comes to me, be vexed?
I don't care! I'll see her standing next
My bed, and hear her voice and touch her dress.
Will she, when she comes, I wonder guess
I'm not *really* thirsty? *I* don't care!
I'll see her face again and smell her hair
As I sit up in bed upon my knees—
Mother! I want a drink of water, please.

20

She's come and gone. She held against my lips
The bedroom glass. I drank it in small sips
To make it last. She said   "Don't call again,
Darling," and smoothed the sheet and counterpane,
Kissed me, and went downstairs again. But oh,
I want her so, I want to see her so!
Mother! Mother! *Mo*-ther! (She's
Coming!) Another drink of water, please!

LIGHT THE LAMPS UP, LAMPLIGHTER

*For a Lamplighter, a Grandmother, The Angel Gabriel
and Any Number of Others*

Light the lamps up, Lamplighter,
The people are in the street—
        Without a light
        They have no sight
And where will they plant their feet?
Some will tread in the gutter,
And some in the mud—oh dear!
Light the lamps up, Lamplighter
Because the night is here.

Light the candles, Grandmother,
The children are going to bed—
        Without a wick
        They'll stumble and stick
And where will they lay their head?
Some will lie on the staircase,
And some in the hearth—oh dear!
Light the candles, Grandmother,
Because the night is here.
Light the stars up, Gabriel,
The cherubs are out to fly—
        If heaven is blind
        How will they find

21

Their way across the sky?
Some will splash in the Milky Way,
Or bump on the moon—oh dear!
Light the stars up, Gabriel,
Because the night is here.

OH, HARK!

O hark, my darling, hark!
I hear the owl in the dark,
The white, low-flying owl
Along the air doth prowl
    With her strange lonely wail.

And hark, my darling, hark!
I hear the stars in the dark,
I hear the singing sky
Shaking with melody!—
    It is the nightingale.

IT WAS LONG AGO

I'll tell you, shall I, something I remember?
Something that still means a great deal to me.
It was long ago.

A dusty road in summer I remember,
A mountain, and an old house and a tree
That stood, you know,

Behind the house. An old woman I remember
In a red shawl with a grey cat on her knee
Humming under a tree.

She seemed the oldest thing I can remember,
But then perhaps I was not more than three.
It was long ago.

I dragged on the dusty road, and I remember
How the old woman looked over the fence at me
And seemed to know

How it felt to be three, and called out, I remember,
"Do you like bilberries and cream for tea?"
I went under the tree

And while she hummed, and the cat purred, I remember
How she filled a saucer with berries and cream for me
So long ago,

Such berries and such cream as I remember
I never had seen before, and never see
Today, you know.

And that is almost all I can remember,
The house, the mountain, the grey cat on her knee,
Her red shawl, and the tree,

And the taste of the berries, the feel of the sun I remember,
And the smell of everything that used to be
So long ago,

Till the heat on the road outside again I remember,
And how the long dusty road seemed to have for me
No end, you know.

That is the farthest thing I can remember.
It won't mean much to you. It does to me.
Then I grew up, you see.

THE TIDE IN THE RIVER

THE TIDE IN THE RIVER

The tide in the river,
The tide in the river,
The tide in the river runs deep.
I saw a shiver
Pass over the river
As the tide turned in its sleep.

SONNETS from FIRST LOVE

Be patient with me. This is still too new...
Oh, if I fail to wear when you are near
The early comradeship, to find the clue
To laughter, to change clouded eyes for clear,
Remember I am going in such a dream
As puts bewilderment upon my days,
And the old habits, an uncaptured stream,
Flow in some outer region seen through haze.
    I will resolve this presently; will learn
    Not to outwear you with this instant mood,
    And loving you, with all my strength will turn
    The loving of you only into good;
    Will hear you laugh, and laugh with you as well,
    And make the time that was, still possible.

I marvel now in what exalted state
Love's truth I fitted to an unfit case.
Only one face of love I knew—too late
I heard that he possessed another face.
I know that when eternal things I sang
Between myself and you, I was misled
By my prevision of a love that sprang
From moods we had not both inhabited.
    Lost friend, it was a mood I could not teach.
    I dreaded to be quick to learn a tongue

24

That offers love the common coin of speech
And leaves the heavenlier air unsung.
Not that I loved too much requires my tears,
I loved too little, and love stopped his ears.

SONNETS from INTERIM

I have found friends such as not many find,
And if I die my friends will grieve indeed,
But I to none of them am so designed
As, gone, to leave his heart in special need.
I see how each one has his own first thought,
And where that first is, nothing is but first—
I may come welcomed, or stand by unsought,
They love not me, as I trust them, with thirst.
    For I make life significant to none,
    I am not any other's share of heaven.
    Must I be glad that when my time is run
    The lives I love will in a day swing even?
    Yes, since I may not look for more—But oh,
    If I should hear one call me as I go!

Certain among us walk in loneliness
Along the pale unprofitable days,
Hazarding many an unanswered guess
At what vague purpose wastes us on our ways.
We know that we are potent to create,
We say, I could be such or such or such,
And lo, indifferent death swings back the gate,
And life has never put us to the touch.
    So women with the aching will to bear
    Still to the barren grave must barren go,
    And men that might again like Titans dare
    Angelic secrets, die and nothing know.
    Alas! why were we born to woe and bliss
    If life had no more need of us than this.

25

I am not very often careless now
With the familiar friends or with the strange,
Though I need never to the new allow
The knowledge that is conscious of a change.
The old are weary that I laugh much less,
The new but find me one who seldom smiles;
I struggle with my constant heaviness
To cheat them into being kind at whiles.
   I must pretend some happiness. So few
   Can long endure even the beloved sad,
   And if they give me up, what will I do?
   Yet how long can I play at being glad?
   It is so strange with friends to act a part,
   And know they hope you will not show your heart.

Yet sometimes still when I am left alone,
And those who love me leave me to myself.
Joy rises like a hero overthrown,
But not yet conquered; joy like a dancing elf
Plays mischief in my veins; joy like a child
Catches at atoms twirling in the light;
Joy like a faun upon the hills runs wild;
Joy like a bird flutters its wings for flight.
   I know him still, the spirit and the fountain!
   He sends all shapes my solitude to fill—
   Joy like a hunter winding on the mountain,
   Joy like a labourer, I know him still!
   And when at night I think my heart is dead,
   Joy like a lover stands beside my bed.

THE REFLECTION

She had no life except to be what men
Required of her to be.
They came for sympathy, and came again
For sympathy.

She never knew the way her heart to spare
When they were hurt or worn.
Whatever one may for another bear
By her was born

They said, you give us of yourself so much!
She heard them with a smile,
Knowing she only gave to such and such
Themselves a while.

Their interests, their frets, their loneliness,
Their sorrows and despairs,
She wore for them—they saw her in no dress
That was not theirs.

She learned to understand the solitudes
When she by none was sought;
Men of themselves grow sick, and in those moods
Needed her not,

Getting relief of others who gave things
By their own purpose lit;
If she too had some freshness in her springs,
None wanted it.

She grew accustomed to be quietly shut
Away, was used to see
Love limping dutifully in a rut
That once ran free;

She knew the signs when friends began to cast
What they had asked her for—
Some asked for much, some little, all at last
Asked nothing more.

And when she died they sorrowed, it is true,
But not for long, because
They had seen some pale reflection that she threw,
Not what she was.

SILENCE

Words and the body always have been much pain to me,
   Little fetters and drags on immensities
   Never to be defined. I am done with these.
Meanings of silence suddenly all grow plain to me.

Something still may sing like a joyous flute in me
   Out of the voice that dares to be voiced aloud,
   But speech no more shall swathe like a burial-shroud
Things unencompassable now eloquent mute in me.

I COME TO WISH

I come to wish I could believe in God,
A God to pray to in my desolation,
A God who owns this spirit and this clod
I call myself, the work of his creation.
I only have a fixed and formless faith
That immortality is in the plan,
That all things do not have an end in death,
And some fine spark outlasts the flesh of man.
   But this I cannot pray to, cannot pray
   Darkly to my own godhead, no, nor even
   To midnight's star, or the gold star of day,
   Hills, trees, or flying birds, or any heaven
   Of high transporting beauty. In my despairs
   I want a listening deity for my prayers.

FOR SHADOWS

When Shadows from the East are long,
Then Larks go up for Morning Song.
When Shadows are not seen at all,

Then Green-Leaves into Silence fall.
When Shadows from the West grow long
Then Blackbirds meet for Evensong.

SONNETS from SECOND LOVE *(to Edward Thomas)*

You seem to me beyond all men to need
The love of men and women, and to have set
The knotted meshes of a stubborn creed
About your spirit like the Roman's net,
Turning your weapon in the circus-ring
Upon the very person of your soul,
And, ere the down-turned thumbs their verdict bring,
Bidding it in the sand self-strangled roll.
  Friend, with the bright and naked blade of love
  In the arena I would be your foe,
  Its edge upon those treacherous toils to prove—
  Yea, though the leaping spirit brought me low
  I would those fetters carve, and then fall down
  While life set on your soul the freedman's crown.

When you are by, what things are said and done,
Or how and in what place, matter no whit,
Whether it be in orchards in the sun
Or small bare chambers by one candle lit,
Whether the mood be set for silence or speech,
And if for speech whether for white or black,
And if for silence whether silence reach
The speechless heart, or frightened falter back.
  It is enough, enough that you are there,
  Beyond all acts and moods it is enough
  That for an instant you are by to share
  The instant in its passage, smooth or rough;
  What shall ensue of it lies out of care—
  Some hurt or some delight? They are one stuff.

Is it a wrong to you, my friend, my friend
Whom I would much more lightly lose than wrong,
At certain times when the unnatural blend
Of love and unfulfilment are too strong,
To set your presence in my empty chair,
Naming dear friendship by its dearer name,
And with an echo fill the vacant air
Of words your lips had never sought to frame?
　　Forgive, forgive the words you have not spoken,
　　Forgive the words I shall not speak to you,
　　Forgive the broken silence, still unbroken,
　　When strength and resolution are worn through!
　　Forgive the looks you are strange to, oh forgive
　　The embrace you will not offer while you live.

A MOTHER TO HER DAUGHTER

She sees me on the eve of love
　　And knows she must not speak,
For I who stand upon the eve
　　Of love, how can I speak?

She sees me fall into my dream
　　With my eyes upon the fire,
And I always come from it to see
　　Her eyes upon the fire.

*In July 1915 Edward Thomas visited Eleanor Farjeon at
Fellows Road, Hampstead, and told her he had joined the
Artists Rifles.*

from SECOND LOVE

Now that you too must shortly go the way
Which in these bloodshot years uncounted men
Have gone in vanishing armies day by day,
And in their numbers will not come again:

I must not strain the moments of our meeting
Striving each look, each accent, not to miss,
Or question of our parting and our greeting—
Is this the last of all? is this—or this?
   Last sight of all it may be with these eyes,
   Last touch, last hearing, since eyes, hands, and ears,
   Even serving love, are our mortalities,
   And cling to what they own in mortal fears:—
   But oh, let end what will, I hold you fast
   By immortal love, which has no first or last.

When we had reached the bottom of the hill
We said farewell, not as it were farewell,
But parting easily, as any will
To whom next day meeting is possible.
Why, it was on a scarcely-finished phrase
We made our clasp, and smiled and turned away—
"I might meet you in London in three days."
The backward look had soon no more to say.
   You might. I thank you that you would not, friend.
   Not thanks for sparing a pain I would have dared,
   But for the change of mind which at the end
   Acknowledged there was something to be spared,
   And parting not so light for you and me
   As you and I made it appear to be.

If you had held me in more tenderness
I think you would have seen me once again;
But had you held me in a little less
Parting would not have stood to you for pain.
And I am glad to know, in leaving me,
One pang you would not face kept us apart,
To set against the mortal agony
I would have gone to meet with all my heart.
   Now I shall always see you on the road
   Turning to wave upon my single call,
   And striding swiftly upward to the wood

While I went swiftly by the village wall,
My spirit singing like a song of praise,
'I might see you in London in three days.'

After Edward Thomas left for France, Eleanor Farjeon went to
stay with Arnold Bax and his wife in Marlow… and recalled.
"It was a week of very thick snow. Very early one morning I
slipped away while the house was still asleep and set out in
the snow for Penn."

ON THE SNOW
January 12 1917, Penn, Buckinghamshire

I knew no woman, child or man
Had been before my steps today.
By Dippel Woods the snow–lanes ran
Soft and uncrushed above their clay;
But little starry feet had traced
Their passages as though in words,
And all those lanes of snow were laced
With runnings of departed birds.

THREE MILES TO PENN

Today I walked three miles to Penn
With an uneasy mind.
The sun shone like a frozen eye,
A light that had gone blind,
The glassy air between the sky
And earth was frozen wind—
All motion and all light again
Were closed within a rind,
As I by wood and field to Penn
Took trouble in my mind.

The slope of cloud in heaven that lay,
Unpeopled hills grown old,
Had no more movement than the land
Locked in a flowing mould;
The sheep like mounds of cloudy sand
Stood soundless in the cold;
There was no stir on all the way
Save what my heart did hold,
So quiet earth and heaven lay,
So quiet and so old.

*When news came of Edward Thomas' death, during the
Battle of Arras, Eleanor went immediately to High Beech,
Loughton, to comfort his widow, Helen.*

THE OUTLET

Grief struck me. I so shook in heart and wit
I thought I must speak of it or die of it.

A certain friend I had with strength to lend,
When mine was spent, I went to find my friend.

Who, rising up with eyes wild for relief,
Hung on my neck and spoke to me of grief.

I raked the ashes of my burned-out strength
And found one coal to warm her with at length.

I sat with her till I was icy cold.
At last I went away, my grief untold.

EASTER MONDAY *(In Memoriam E.T.)*

In the last letter that I had from France
You thanked me for the silver Easter egg
Which I had hidden in the box of apples
You liked to munch beyond all other fruit.
You found the egg the Monday before Easter
And said, 'I will praise Easter Monday now—
It was such a lovely morning.'   Then you spoke
Of the coming battle and said, 'This is the eve.
Good-bye. And may I have a letter soon.'

That Easter Monday was a day for praise,
It was such a lovely morning. In our garden
We sowed our earliest seeds, and in the orchard
The apple bud was ripe. It was the eve.
There are three letters that you will not get.

April 9th 1917

PEACE

I.

I am as awful as my brother War,
I am the sudden silence after clamour.
I am the face that shows the seamy scar
When blood has lost its frenzy and its glamour.
Men in my pause shall know the cost at last
That is not to be paid in triumphs or tears,
Men will begin to judge the thing that's past
As men will judge it in a hundred years.

Nations! whose ravenous engines must be fed
Endlessly with the father and the son,
My naked light upon your darkness, dread!—
By which ye shall behold what ye have done:
Whereon, more like a vulture than a dove,
Ye set my seal in hatred, not in love.

II.

Let no man call me good. I am not blest.
My single virtue is the end of crimes,
I only am the period of unrest,
The ceasing of the horrors of the times;
My good is but the negative of ill,
Such ill as bends the spirit with despair,
Such ill as makes the nations' soul stand still
And freeze to stone beneath its Gorgon glare.

Be blunt, and say that peace is but a state
Wherein the active soul is free to move,
And nations only show as mean or great
According to the spirit then they prove—
O which of ye whose battle-cry is Hate
Will first in peace dare shout the name of Love?

THE NIGHT WILL NEVER STAY

The night will never stay,
The night will still go by,
Though with a million stars
You pin it to the sky,
Though you bind it with the blowing wind
And buckle it with the moon,
The night will slip away,
Like sorrow or a tune.

THE GIFT OF ENGLISH WORDS

ALPHABET

One letter stands for Alphabet
  And Alphabet stands for all,
There's six-and-twenty in the set
  By which we stand or fall.
And most of us know in our head
Their rightful order, A to Z.

But when we take the Alphabet
  To pieces, and spell words,
The little letters, all upset,
  Fly anywhere, like birds.
Why, ALPHABET itself gets mixed,
And when you spell it, comes unfixed.

For then L follows after A,
  And H comes after P,
And T turns tail and runs away
  To hob-a-nob with E.
You all can *say* your Alphabet—
But, children, can you spell it yet?

> *"Choose me,*
> *You English words….." Edward Thomas*

ENGLISH

As gardens grow with flowers
English grows with words,
Words that have secret powers,
Words that give joy like birds.

Some of the words you say,
Both in and out of school,
Are brighter than the day
And deeper than a pool.

Some words there are that dance,
Some words there are that sigh,
The fool's words come by chance,
The poet's to heaven fly.

When you are grown, your tongue
Should give the joy of birds;
Get while you are young
The gift of English words.

MARY INDOORS

Aren't you coming out, Mary?
  Come out, your eyes will tire—
Oh, let me be, please, please, said she,
  I want to read by the fire.

What are you reading, Mary,
  That keeps you, keeps you in?
Oh, wonderful things of knights and kings,
  With their heart's desire to win.

Look out of the window, Mary!
  The blustering day is bright.
Come fight the wind with us, and find
  The sun on the hilly height.

Come on out of it, Mary,
  And win your heart's desire!—
Oh, let me be, please, *please,* said she,
  I want to read by the fire.

KNOWLEDGE

Your mind is a meadow
To plant for your needs;
You are the farmer
With knowledge for seeds.

Don't leave your meadow
Unplanted and bare,
Sow it with knowledge
And tend it with care.

Who'd be a know-nothing
When he might grow
The seed of the knowledge
Of stars and of snow;

The science of numbers,
The stories of time,
The magic of music,
The secrets of rhyme?

Don't be a know-nothing!
Plant in the spring,
And see what a harvest
The summer will bring.

LATIN

When Julius Caesar was a child
In Rome, the same things drove him wild
        As now in England fidget us.
He blubbered in the Latin tongue:
"*Mater,* a naughty *Apis* stung
        Me here, upon the *Digitus!*"
(By which he meant: "A naughty Bee
Has stung my finger, Mother, see!")

His *Mater* took him on her knees,
And cooed: "Those horrid little Bees!
　　　Now why did Jove invent 'em?"
And then she calmed her *Filius*
And put upon his *Digitus*
　　　A soothing Unguentum
(Which means she smeared an ointment on
The finger of her little son.)

At tea, to make her Julius well,
She gave him *Panis,* spread with *Mel*—
　　　(And if you think that's funny,
It only means *your* Mother might
Console you for an insect-bite
　　　At tea with Bread-and-Honey).
Now, Honey's such a pleasant thing
He quite forgot his *Apis* sting.

Though Julius Caesar lived in Rome
And you inside a British home,
　　　You're very like that brat in
The things he said when he was young,
Though you speak in the English tongue,
　　　And Julius spoke in Latin.
So when you say a Latin word
That is the one which Caesar heard.

ORNITHOLOGY

What's ORNITHOLOGY? Pray can you tell?
It's hard to pronounce and it's harder to spell—
Yet that's what you're learning whenever you care
To study the Birds of the Earth, Sea and Air.
　　　　There's a long word
　　　　To stand for a Bird!
For a Lark or a Sparrow it's length is absurd!

Eagles and Ostriches need no apology
If you should label them as ORNITHOLOGY!
But how can it fit
The tiny Tom-Tit?
The Finch
Wants a word that's no more than an inch!
Yet all of the Birds of the East and the West,
Whatever they be, and wherever they nest—
The Vulture—the Hen—
The Flamingo—the Wren—
The Dove—the Canary—
The queer Cassowary—
The Thrush on the bough, and the Duck in the pool—
They are all ORNITHOLOGY when you're in School!

POETRY

What is Poetry? Who knows?
Not the rose, but the scent of the rose,
Not the sky, but the light in the sky,
Not the fly, but the gleam of the fly;
Not the sea, but the sound of the sea,
Not myself, but what makes me
See, hear and feel something that prose
Cannot; and what it is, who knows?

MARY'S ONE

Do you write one every day? said Mary.
Well, I said, I try.
Then will you write one for me? said Mary.
That I will, said I.

I went with Mary to find a ball—

And we never found it;
To look for a thrush's nest—and all
    We saw were the hedge-leaves round it;

To see a wagtail on a pond—
    But we couldn't catch it;
And a water-lily that grew beyond—
    Too far for us to snatch it;

To watch for rabbits in a grove
    At play on a sandbank sunny—
But I was born as blind as love,
    And never saw one bunny.

After that I wrote Mary one
    In less than half a minute—
And now that Mary's one is done
    I see there's nothing in it.

PEGASUS

From the blood of Medusa
Pegasus sprang
His hoof upon heaven
Like melody rang,
His whinny was sweeter
Than Orpheus' lyre,
The wing on his shoulder
Was brighter than fire.

His tail was a fountain,
His nostrils were caves,
His mane and his forelock
Were musical waves,
He neighed like a trumpet,
He cooed like a dove,

He was stronger than terror
And swifter than love.

He could not be captured,
He could not be bought,
His running was rhythm,
His standing was thought;
With one eye on sorrow
And one eye on mirth,
He galloped in heaven
And gambolled on earth.

And only the poet
With wings to his brain
Can mount him and ride him
Without any rein,
The stallion of heaven,
The steed of the skies,
The horse of the singer
Who sings as he flies.

*(Pegasus is the winged horse of the Gods in Greek
mythology and an inspiration for Music and Poetry)*

BOOKS

What worlds of wonder are our books!
As one opens them and looks
New ideas and people rise
In our fancies and our eyes.

The room we sit in melts away,
And we find ourselves at play
With someone who, before the end,
May become our chosen friend.

Or we sail along the page
To some other land or age.
Here's our body in the chair,
But our mind is over *there*.

Each book is a magic box
Which with a touch a child unlocks.
In between their outside covers
Books hold all things for their lovers.

ROOM FOR ANOTHER ONE

MRS MALONE

Mrs Malone
Lived hard by a wood,
All on her lonesome
As nobody should,
With her crust on a plate
And her pot on the coal
And none but herself
To converse with, poor soul.
In a shawl and a hood
She got sticks out-of-door,
On a bit of old sacking
She slept on the floor,
And nobody, nobody,
Asked how she fared
Or knew how she managed,
For nobody cared.
   Why make a pother
   About an old crone?
   What for should they bother
   With Mrs. Malone?

One Monday in winter
With snow on the ground
So thick that a footstep
Fell without sound,
She heard a faint frostbitten
Peck on the pane
And went to the window
To listen again.
There sat a cock-sparrow
Bedraggled and weak,
With half-open eyelid
And ice on his beak.
She threw up the sash
And she took the bird in
And mumbled and fumbled it

Under her chin.
   "Ye're all of a smother,
    Ye're fair overblown!
    I've room fer another,"
    Said Mrs Malone.

Come Tuesday while eating
Her dry morning slice
With the sparrow a-picking
("Ain't company nice!")
She heard on her doorstep
A curious scratch,
And there was a cat
With its claw on the latch.
It was hungry and thirsty
And thin as a lath,
It mewed and it mowed
On the slithery path.
She threw the door open
And warmed up some pap,
And huddled and cuddled it
In her old lap.
   "There, there, little brother,
    Ye poor skin-an'-bone,
    There's room fer another,"
    Said Mrs Malone.

Come Wednesday while all of them
Crouched on the mat
With a crumb for the sparrow,
A sip for the cat,
There was wailing and whining
Outside in the wood,
And there sat a vixen
With six of her brood.
She was haggard and ragged
And worn to a shred,
And her half-dozen babies

Were only half-fed,
But Mrs Malone, crying
"My! Ain't they sweet!"
Happed them and lapped them
And gave them to eat.
  "You warm yerself, mother,
   Ye're cold as a stone!
   There's room fer another."
   Said Mrs. Malone.

Come Thursday a donkey
Stepped in off the road
With sores on her withers
From bearing a load.
Come Friday when icicles
Pierced the white air
Down from the mountainside
Lumbered a bear.
For each she had something
If little, to give—
"Lord knows, the poor critters
Must all of 'em live."
She gave them her sacking,
Her hood and her shawl,
Her loaf and her teapot—
She gave them her all!
  "What with one thing and t'other
  Me fambily's grown,
  And there's room fer another,"
  Said Mrs. Malone.

Come Saturday evening
When time was to sup
Mrs. Malone
Had forgot to sit up.
The cat said *meeow,*
And the sparrow said *peep,*
The vixen, *she's sleeping,*

The bear, *let her sleep.*
On the back of the donkey
They bore her away,
Through trees and up mountains
Beyond night and day,
Till come Sunday morning
They brought her in state
Through the last cloudbank
As far as the Gate.
"Who is it?" asked Peter,
"You have with you there?"
And donkey and sparrow,
Cat, vixen and bear

Exclaimed "Do you tell us
Up here she's unknown?
It's our mother, God bless us!
It's Mrs Malone
Whose havings were few
And whose holding was small
And whose heart was so big
It had room for us all."
Then Mrs Malone
Of a sudden awoke,
She rubbed her two eyeballs
And anxiously spoke:
"Where am I, to goodness,
And what do I see?
My dears, let's turn back,
This ain't no place fer me!"
But Peter said "Mother
Go in to the Throne
There's room for another
One, Mrs Malone."

CATS

Cats sleep
Anywhere.
Any table,
Any chair,
Top of piano,
Window-ledge,
In the middle,
On the edge,
Open drawer,
Empty shoe,
Anybody's
Lap will do,
Fitted in a
Cardboard box,
In the cupboard
With your frocks,
Anywhere!
They don't care!
Cats sleep anywhere.

THE GOLDEN CAT

My golden cat had dappled sides;
No prince has worn so fine a cloak;
Patterned like sea-water where rides
The sun, or like the flower in oak

Where the rough plank has been planed out,
Lovely as yellow mackerel skies
In moonlight, or a speckled trout.
Clear as swung-honey were his eyes.

It was a wondrous daily thing
To look for, when his beautiful
Curved body gathered for a spring
That, light as any golden gull,

Flashed over the fine net of wire
Which my casement window bars;
His leap was bright as tongues of fire,
And swift as autumn shooting stars.

My cat was like a golden gift,
A golden myth of Grecian lore—
But things so bright, and things so swift,
Must vanish, and he is no more.

MR SHERATON'S CAT

Mr Sheraton had a cat,
I'm certain of that.

Mr Sheraton's cat's
Pats
Posed so prettily on the floor—
Two behind and two before,
While Puss herself demurely stood
Graceful, proportioned, perfect, good—
That Mr. Sheraton eyeing the sweet
Turn of those small fastidious feet,
Cried: "Eureka! at last I'm able
To turn the legs of my chair and table!"
Men praised his work then and thereafter.

The feline race subdues its laughter,
And gazes down its exquisite legs
To its turned out pads that can walk on eggs,
Purrs: "Mr Sheraton's credit? *That's*
Mr Sheraton's cat's".

TO CONEY: MY KITTEN
(A Poem Under Difficulties)

Kitten like a ball of gold,
Not much more than ten weeks old,
Must you really try to bite
My penholder as I write?
Must you really cut up capers
All along my notes and papers?
Must you really, do you think,
Dip your tail into my ink
And on my tale wipe it dry?
Do you really have to try
Making a duet of it
While I type-write, golden kit?
Kitten! that's my pencil, please!
Kitten! those are my two knees!
Kitten! why by all the laws,
Have you pins instead of claws?
Kitten! I am not a tree—
Don't come clambering up me!
Go away, you little blighter!
You're a kitten, I'm a writer,
And if you my verses chew,
How can I buy milk for you?
Did you hear me? Go away!...

Oh, all right, then. Stay and play.

DOG

Whether I'm Alsatian,
Dachshund or Dalmatian,
Or any one among the terrier crew,
However brief you've known me,
As long as you will own me,
I'm Dog, that's all, my Master, Dog to you!

If you like a setter
Or a Spaniel better,
Aberdeen or Airedale— some folk do —
Whatever breed you name me
As long as you will claim me
I'm yours for life, my Master, Dog to you.

I'll love you, Cairn or Collie,
Beyond the point of folly,
And if I'm Mongrel, love you just as true.
Kick me or caress me,
As long as you possess me
I'm yours till death, my Master, Dog to you.

For you, I'll be so knowing!
I'll whimper at your going,
And at your coming wag myself in two!
Trust you while I tease you,
Pester you to please you,
Your dog, that's all, Master, Dog to you.

INSIDE

A bellyful and the fire,
And him in his old suit,
And me with my heart's desire,
My head across his foot.

And I doze. And he reads.
And the clock ticks slow.
And, though he never heeds,
He knows, and I know.

Presently, without look,
His hand will feel to tug
My ear, his eyes on book,
Mine upon the rug.

NOTHING

He's gone—
     and there is nothing.
Kind tones
     are nothing,
The next-door cat
     is nothing,
Even his empty gloves and hat
     are nothing,
The fighters in the street
     are nothing,
Friends, foes, and meat
     are nothing, nothing, nothing—
He's gone,
     and I am nothing.

EPITAPH

What is this Stone he's laid upon my bones
For whom I fetched and carried endless stones?
Wait, Master, wait a little. When we meet
You'll know me by my Stone, laid at your feet.

DIVERSIONS

from THE ABC of the BBC

I announce: The Announcer! Don't ask me his name,
    He's the Voice in the air, he's the Call
That all British Listeners greet with the same
    Attention in cottage and hall.

He's the Signal for which every ear is in tune,
    He's the Rocket that soars in the night
And heralds the stars that will burst on us soon,
    And call forth our "Ohs!" of delight.

He's the Rise of the Curtain that shows us the Play
    Which makes us now laugh and now cry—
Hush! don't miss a word he's preparing to say!
    It's the B.B.C. calling! Stand by!

B is for BIG BEN

Time for the Time Signal!
    Speak, Big Ben!
Boom out the time
    To children and men,
Over Great Britain's
    Listening Isles,
Send your voice ringing
    For miles upon miles.
Children that listen
    Will turn into men
Ere you cease telling the
    Time, Big Ben.
Men that now hear you
    Tell the time plain,
Ere you are dumb will be
    Children again.
Britain is listening,
    Wondering…When?

Time for the Time Signal—
   Speak, Big Ben!

J IS FOR JAZZ

The Jazz is on in the West End—
   Sing hey! for the gay Savoy!
Before the musical jest end,
   Switch on the Wireless, boy!

The others may pay their guinea
   To go to the dance to-night,
But I in my working pinny
   Will foot it with you as light.

The others may do it in style, and
   Eat caviare with their fizz,
But the dance goes all over the island,
   Wherever the Wireless is.

Yes, the Wireless end is the best end
   For every girl and boy
When the Jazz is on in the West-End—
   Sing hey! for the gay Savoy!

L IS FOR LICENCE

I saw a blithe maiden go skipping so gay,
"Whither away, maiden, whither away?"
         "Kind sir, I must go
         To the nearest P.O."
(She answered), "with ten silver shillings to pay,
For a Licence costs only ten shillings, you know,
A Licence costs less than a penny a day!"

"And what do you get for your Licence, my dear?"
"A dance and a song and a laugh and a tear,
        Wisdom and folly
        And sweet melancholy,"
(She answered), "by turns in the pageant appear.
I can keep my thoughts fresh, I can keep my heart jolly,
All for the sum of ten shillings a year!"

"Maiden, is that why you skip on your way?"
"Why, who wouldn't skip, and who wouldn't be gay?
        The shillings aren't many,
        The troubles not any"
(She answered), "and think of the wondrous array
Of treats that they give you for three days a penny,
Ten shillings a year, not a ha'penny a day!"

N IS FOR NEWS BULLETIN

News, News, all the News!
I will tell it in two twos!
Politics and Art and Sport,
All the News of every sort!
Weddings, Science and Finance,
What they're doing out in France,
What they're saying out in Spain,
I will tell it all again!
Fall in Sugar, rise in Corn,
Who is dead and who is born,
What the weather's going to be,
You shall hear it all from me.
News at Seven o'clock and Ten,
News of Mice and News of Men,
News that gladdens and appals,
Accidents and Festivals,
News of Trains, and News of Ships,
News of Courts, and Aerial Trips,

News of new Discoveries,
News of everything there is—
If you'll only listen in,
Friends, to the News Bulletin,
You shall hear it in two twos,
News, News, all the News!

P IS FOR PROGRAMMES

When the boy brings the papers on Friday
At eight as the breakfast–bell chimes,
    The Family burst
    Down the stairs to be first
To get at The *Radio Times!*
And the lucky one turning the pages
Is hailed by the rest of them—"Speak!
    Now don't be unfair,
    Let us all have a share—
Come! what are the programmes this week?"
        "Well—
    On Friday you shall hear a Play,
    On Saturday you'll dance so gay,
    On Sunday there's a Poet who
    Will come to read to me and you,
    On Monday there's a Humorist
    Who certainly must not be missed,
    On Tuesday there's a Concert, and
    On Wednesday there's a famous Band,
    On Thursdays there's a special Star
    To talk to us— and there you are!
    The Programmes in their full array
    Have something good for every day.
        And—
On Friday the boy with the papers
Will come as the breakfast-bell chimes,
    While the Family burst
    Down the stairs to be first
To get at *The Radio Times!*

Q IS FOR QUESTIONS

There isn't a question
Abroad in the air
That doesn't get broadcast
While lingering there.
There isn't a question
On Art or Finance
That Broadcasting doesn't
Take in at a glance.
There isn't a question
Of any old sort,
On Music or Politics,
Science or Sport,
That doesn't immediate
Interest win
For anyone given
To Listening-In.
Yes, every known Question
Let nobody doubt it,
Is Broadcast to-day,
There's no Question about it!

Under the pseudonym Tomfool, Eleanor Farjeon wrote for the Daily Herald during the First World War, contributing witty, topical verses based on current news items. These were popular with readers, who only discovered the author's real name after two small collections, Tomfooleries and Moonshine appeared in the 1920's. A medieval jester in scarlet and yellow danced on the covers, illustrated by Macdonald Gill.

PREFERENCES

(From a recent public speech on dress by a lady: "I prefer the nude when it is draped.")

I prefer an angry uncle when he's placid,
    I prefer a cup of cocoa when it's tea,
I prefer a game of Whist when it is Auction,
    And I prefer two shillings when they're three.

I prefer Virginian fags when they are Turkish,
    I prefer to sleep in blankets when they're sheets,
I *much* prefer a bee when it's a blue-bottle,
    I prefer an ode by Swinburne when it's Keats.

I prefer most things when they are something different—
    Yet the argument *au fond* is rather crude;
You *can't* prefer the nude when it is draped, ma'am,
    Because when it is draped it isn't nude.

REFLECTIONS ON TWO PINS

Are the things men are eager to do for Two
        Pins
            Ever Done?
And what would the Chap who to do them

   begins
     Do for *One?*
For Two he is equal to punching my head,
    So he swears;
For Two he will kick me, he's frequently said
    Down the stairs;
For two knock me flat till I tumble, a wreck,
    In a heap;
Or he will, with great pleasure, for Two,
    wring my neck—
     It seems cheap.
Still, I'll *keep* my Two Pins, and his boast,
    false or true,
     Passes me—
But what would The Chap who does these
    things for Two,
     Do for *Three!*

RANDOM REFLECTIONS ON A PARK SEAT

(When Park Seats were put up to Twopence)

They charge now in the Royal Parks in town
Twopence, and not two halfpence to sit down.

I wonder, since it never rains, but pours,
If it's a bob to go down on all fours—

Or if it would cost more than half-a-crown
An hour to take existence lying down?

Of course, while prices rise and incomes fall,
It's cheaper never to be born at all;

But since we *are* born—let us try to meet
The cost while standing on our own two feet.

THE PERFECTION OF THE STRANGER

The Perfection of the Stranger
Is a mystery to us all—
It's the one sort of Perfection
That is never known to pall.
No doubts beset our confidence,
No fears our bosoms thrill,
Whilst the Stranger who is Perfect
Remains Strange and Perfect still.

Why is the Stranger Perfect?
By what ungenerous laws
Are Bosom-Friends and Blood-Brothers
So full of flecks and flaws?
I wonder if some new light
On the question would descend
If one man's Perfect Stranger
Were another's Bosom-Friend?

Ah! let us probe no further
That which heaven has disguised!
Let the Stranger's Strange Perfection
Stay unpsycho-analysed—
Lest we find that every vision
Of perfection out of range
Becomes at once Imperfect
When it ceases to be Strange.

A LULLABY IN LINGERIE

("Gentlemen's Slumber Suits"
Announcement in a West End shop window)

Sleep, Gentlemen, sleep!
Dream, Lady, dream!
Time for you to go to bed,
Stars are in the sky—
One in a Slumber-Suit
That is the Final Scream,
The other in a Doze-Dress
That is the Latest Cry.

Put your Twilight Toilet by,
Midnight is at hand;
Lay aside your Wander-Wear
In a little heap—
Slumber-Suit and Doze-Dress
And moonlight on the land—
Dream, Lady, Dream!
Sleep, Gentleman, Sleep!

GLOSSARY
Slumber-Suit—Pyjamas
Doze-Dress—Nightdress
Twilight Toilet—Evening
Dress
Wander-Wear—Walking
Costume

THE IMMORTAL MOTLEY

"Are lovers of Shakespeare to tolerate a shabby Julius
Caesar or a moth-eaten Hamlet on account of the high
price of material for the stage costumes?" asks a daily
paper, reporting the efforts of the "Old Vic" to establish a
good stock Shakespearian wardrobe.)

Time the moth may spoil their gowns,
    Time the thief may pick their gems,
Time the rust may prove their crowns
    Tarnished tinsel diadems:
But what, sweet Will, hath Time to do with thee
Who dressed thy people in eternity?

Shabby Shakespeare? Nay, I swear,
   Hamlet, that thy sable cloth
Can resist the wear and tear
   Of time, the rust, the thief, the moth;
And none but he that hath a shabby mind
In any guise will Shakespeare shabby find.

RAVENOUS JUSTICE

("There is nothing worse than a starving Judge"…
*   Judge Cluer, on adjourning for luncheon)*

Nothing is worse than a starving Judge….
For only suppose the judge unfed!
He might, poor fellow, in error smudge
The laws of the land, and lose his head.

He might be tempted to steal a ham,
Or sausages made of cow or pig,
Conceal in his gown a pot of jam,
Or hide a kipper under his wig.

And what, oh what, would the court believe
If he sentenced Bill Jones for pinching a purse
And a bun dropped out of his lordship's sleeve?
Frankly, I ask you, what could be worse?

Then, lest Dame Justice should suffer abuse,
A meal to the Woolsack let no man grudge—
For a starving tramp there is some excuse,
But *nothing* is worse than a starving Judge.

AN EXPOSURE OF THE CREEPS

("Hansard is wonderfully accurate, and when a mistake does creep into its pages..." Daily Paper)

Writhing their way on their stomachs,
Worming their way o'er the ground,
   Towards every sort
   Of public Report
The Mistakes *will* come creeping around.
They never stride in, you may notice,
With a blatant and obvious din,
   But down on all fours
   O'er the printing–house floors,
The mistakes creep insidiously in.

You may guard your Report like an Argus,
You may put your Report on the chain,
   Build a wall topped with spikes,
   Such as nobody likes,
To protect your Report, and in vain!
The moment you flicker an eyelash
A rustling is sure to begin
   By the double-barred gate
   Where Mistakes lie in wait
To take their first chance to creep in.

Have you ever yet seen one that strutted?
Or that breasted the wind as it ran?
   Or as it advanced
   That hopped, skipped or danced?
Or even walked in like a man?
No! like mice and like beetles and shadows,
Through some crack in the printing-house doors,
   While the Staff sweetly sleeps
   The Mistake creeps... and creeps...
And does in the Report to its snores.

TREE–LAW

*(An ex-soldier was stated, at Highgate Police Court, to
have been found holding conversation with a tree. The
sequel was a fine of 10 shillings—Daily Paper)*

I often have exchanged a speech
About the weather with a beech,
Or paused to crack a jolly joke
In hearty converse with an oak,
Or chattered airy balderdash
With some young feather-minded ash,
Or lightly passed the time o'morn
At daybreak with a budding thorn.
At twilight with a silver birch
I've held poetical research;
I've often thanked a white-backed beam,
A poplar told me once its dream;
To one elm's heart I've opened mine,
And talked of heaven with a pine.
What conscience-money do I owe
The State for having transgressed so?
Sirs, fine this poor soul as ye will,
He must with trees be talking still,
And praise his God, who hath no whim
To fine the trees that talked to him.

THE DULL SIDE OF THINGS

I did not care in the days gone by
Whether a Match was one day or three—
Under drizzling rain or a dreary sky,
Cricket was never too dull for me.

I was willing to wait an hour in queue,
And when I got in behold C.B.

64

Decide that they wouldn't begin till Two—
Cricket was never too dull for me.

I was willing to sit for half a day
With a bag of buns and a flask of tea,
And not a prospect of morning play—
Cricket was never too dull for me.

I was willing to feel the hard hard seat
Grow harder than wood is supposed to be,
While pins and needles assailed my feet—
But cricket was never too dull for me.

And when after hours the play began,
And Barnes took Seven for Forty-Three,
And I yelled with the Crowd as a single man—
Cricket was *never* too dull for me!

THE GAME THAT'S NEVER DONE

Soft, soft, the sunset falls upon the pitch,
The game is over and the stumps are drawn,
The willow sleeps in its appointed niche,
The heavy roller waits another dawn—
    Bowled is the final ball again,
    Hushed is the umpire's call again,
The fielders and the batsmen cease to run—
    But memory will play again
    Many and many a day again
The game that's done, the game that's never done.

In happy dreams we'll see each ball rebowled,
And mend the fault that robbed us of some prize,
In dreams we'll hold the catch we failed to hold,
And see our duck's eggs swell to centuries—
    In dreams we'll take the field again,

In dreams the willow wield again,
And set the red ball spinning in the sun—
    Ah, memory will play again
    Many and many a day again
The game that's done, the game that's never done.

(Written in collaboration with her brother Herbert Farjeon for his anthology 'Cricket Bag')

from THE TOWN CHILD'S ALPHABET

F is for FLOWER-SELLER

The Flower-seller's fat and she wears a big shawl,
She sits on the kerb with her basket and all,
The wares that she sells us are not very dear,
And are always the loveliest things of the year.
         Daffodils in April,
         Purple Flags in May,
         Sweet Peas like butterflies
         Upon a summer day,
         Brown leaves in autumn,
         Green leaves in spring,
         And berries in the winter
         When the carol-singers sing.
The Flower-seller sits with her hands in her lap,
When she's not crying Roses she's taking a nap,
Her bonnet is queer, and she calls you My Dear,
And sells you the loveliest things of the year.

J is for JAZZ-MAN

      Crash   and
              CLANG!
      Bash   and
              BANG!
And up in the road the Jazz-Man sprang!
The One-Man-Jazz-Band playing in the street,
Drums with his Elbows, Cymbals with his Feet,
Pipes with his Mouth, Accordian with his Hand,
Playing all his Instruments to Beat the Band!
      TOOT   and
              Tingle!
      HOOT   and
              Jingle!

Oh, what a Clatter! how the tunes all mingle!
Twenty Children couldn't make as much Noise as
The Howling Pandemonium of the One-Man-Jazz!

P is for POLICEMAN

The dangers of the Strand
    Obey the Policeman's Will,
The Policeman lifts his hand
    And London all stands still.

No single word is said,
    But when the danger's gone
The Policeman nods his head
    And London all moves on.

Q is for QUEUE-GIRL

Whether it shines or snows or pours,
The Queue-girl at the theatre doors
Takes up her stand and waits all day
To get a good seat for the play.

She eats, to while away the wait,
Ham sandwiches and chocolate,
And reads a book, and knits a sock,
And frequently consults the clock.

And kindly people come along
To play a tune or sing a song,
Or show off any gift they've got
To help the Queue-girl bear her lot.

R is for ROADMENDER

Where the buses and cabs are so thick
  That they've cracked the poor road into two,
The Roadmender comes with his pick
  To patch up the damage they do.

He ropes off a bit of the street,
  The bit that amuses him best,
And then he has something to eat,
  And leans on his spade for a rest.

He takes up a square block of wood,
  And pauses his forehead to wipe,
And then has a bite more of food
  And then takes a pull at his pipe.

He looks at the hole he has made
  And thoughtfully scratches his head,
And, stacking his pick and his spade,
  Goes home to his supper and bed.

T IS FOR TAXI-MAN

The Taxi-Man is a go-ahead man,
  And a little bit of a swank;
He keeps his cab as smart as he can,
  And he never forgets his rank.

U IS FOR UNCLE

Uncle is the sort of man
  Who comes at an unusual time
And calls out, "Hallo, Kiddies! Can
  You take me to the Pantomime"

69

The play's no sooner over than
   He bellows very heartily
"Well, what about it, Kiddies? Can
   You manage ices for your tea?"

And without any previous plan,
   When taking leave, as like as not
He chinks his pockets, shouting "Can
   You spend five shillings, Kiddies, what?"

Uncle is that sort of man,
And as for Us, of course we can!

W is for WAITRESS

Waitress, please to wait on me;
Milk for one and tea for two,
Toast for me and buns for you,
Bread and butter brown and white
Queen-cake sweet and sponge-cake light,
Coffee éclair, creamy puff—
Yes, I think that's quite enough.
Pleasant waitress, deft and neat,
Nimble-fingered, quick of feet,
What's the reckoning? Two-and-three.
Thank you, Waitress, for our tea.

from A SUSSEX ALPHABET

ARUNDEL

Run, Aran, run and tell,
How shall men know Arundel?
A Castle Tower, a Cathedral Bell,
By these all men know Arundel.

BELLOC

Mr Belloc lives in Sussex
And don't you dare to doubt it!
He makes good cheer and drinks good beer,
And tells us all about it.

LONG MAN OF WILMINGTON

You Long Long Man of Wilmington
How long have you been there?—
Before your grandsire's grandsire's grandsire's
Grandsire's sire was seen there.

You Long Long Man of Wilmington,
How long will you be there?—
Until your grandson's grandson's grandson's
Grandson's son see me there.

RYE

Mermaid, Mermaid in the Rye,
On the hill left high and dry,
How much happier you would be
Swimming in the Winchelsea.

UCKFIELD

I went to Uckfield to swim in the sea,
But when I got there it was dry as could be.
'To Cuckfield, to Cuckfield!' a Cuckooo told me,
'For Cuckfield is Uckfield, you know, with a C.'

But Cuckfield was dry as a six-year-old pea,
So I went back to Uckfield as quick as could be.
I ducked in the grass and I dived from a tree,
And the Cuckoo of Uckfield cried 'Cuckoo!' at me.

ALL THE WAY TO ALFRISTON

All the way to Alfriston,
From Chichester to Alfriston,
I went along the running Downs
High above the patchwork plain,
Fantastical as Joseph's coat
With coloured squares of grass and grain,
Earthen russets, duns and browns,
Charlock-yellow, clover-green,
Reddening wheat and silvery oat:
And rivers coiling in between
And roofs of little peopled towns.

I heard the wind among the leaves
And corn that was not yet in sheaves
Swishing with the sound of surf;
I heard the cry of distant trains,
The rush and drip of scudding rains,
I heard my foot-beat on the turf,
The lark's delight, the pewit's plaint,
Hoarse calls of shepherds, bark and bleat,
Sheep-bells and church-bells in the heat,
And rambling thunders, far and faint:
And I saw dew-ponds round as pearls,
And multitudes of summer flowers,
Mulleins tall as little girls,
And Canterbury Bells in showers,
Fields flushed with sainfoin, banks that blazed
With golden toad-flax and such fires
Of poppy that I was amazed;
And chicory as blue as heaven
Seen in clear water: I saw spires,
And thatches, castles, barns and towers,
The furnace of a clinking forge
And bridges made of wood and stone;
And by an ancient hostel even
Saw demons in the open street,
A rabbit at a Bishop's feet,

Angels and dragons and Saint George,
When I was come to Alfriston.

I ate my bread on open places,
I 'changed a smile with many faces,
I loved the jokes and commerce with
The jolly baker and the smith,
The gypsy with her wheedling eyes,
Her pack of wares, her pack of lies;
I loved the rain-storms and the sun,
The silent shepherds, young and old,
I loved the cropping wandering fold,
The silky dog that chased the sheep,
I loved my rest when day was done,
I loved the Downs, awake, asleep,
All the way to Alfriston,
From Chichester to Alfriston.

from NURSERY RHYMES of LONDON TOWN

KING'S CROSS

King's Cross!
What shall we do?
His purple robe
Is rent in tow!
Out of his Crown
He's torn the Gems!
He's thrown his Sceptre
        Into the Thames!
        The Court is shaking
        In its shoe—
        King's Cross!
        What shall we do?
        Leave him alone for a minute or two.

THE STOCK EXCHANGE

There's a Bull and a Bear, and what do you think?
They live in a Garden of white Stocks and pink.
"I'll give you a pink stock for one of your white,"
Says the Bear to the Bull, and the Bull says "All Right!"
They never make answer if anyone knocks,
They are always so busy exchanging their Stocks.

SHEPHERD'S BUSH

O if you go to London Town you'll find a
    Shepherd there
Who sits beneath a Hawthorn Bush and pipes a
    sylvan air;
And little bleating kids and woolly lambkins
    crowd and push
To dance and prance of a May Morning around
    the Shepherd's Bush.

BATTERSEA

Little boy, little boy, what is the matter?
Madam, the sea has been turned into batter!

Little boy, little boy, what does it matter?
Madam, I cannot go swimming in batter.

Little boy, little boy, that's no great matter!—
Madam, how *shall* I get rid of the batter?

Why, with your spoon and your fork and your platter, see,
Little boy, little boy, eat up the Batter-sea!

HAMMERSMITH

Hammer, Smith! hammer, Smith!
    What will you shoe my pony with?
        I'll shoe it with a shoe of steel,
        Another of gold so red,
        A third shoe of ivory,
        And a fourth shoe of lead.
Then I'll pay you with a brass farthing
I picked up out of the roadway,
So hammer, Smith! hammer, Smith!
For I want to ride down the Broadway.

KENSAL RISE

Kensal is a Sleepy-head—
    Run and pull her out of bed!
Five o'clock and six are gone,
Lazy Kensal slumbers on;
Seven has struck and eight is past,
Kensal still is snoring fast,
While her angry Mistress cries:
"Get up, Kensal! Kensal, rise!"

THE ANGEL

    The Angel flew down
    One morning to town
But didn't know where to rest,
For they shut her out of the East End
And they shut her out of the West.

    The Angel went on
    To Islington,
And there the people were kinder.
If ever you go to Islington
That's where you will find her.

FLEET STREET

In Fleet Street, in Fleet Street, the people are so fleet
They barely touch the cobble-stones with their nimble feet!
The Lads run like a windy day, the Lasses run like rain,
From Temple Bar to Ludgate Hill, and then run back again.

OXFORD CIRCUS

The Circus has come from Oxford City
With Ponies and Jugglers and Ladies so pretty,
Pay up your pennies and don't be shirkers—
All the Fun of the Fair is at Oxford Circus!

WORMWOOD SCRUBS

Wormwood scrubs, Wormwood scrubs,
    Windows, walls, and floors,
Pots and pans and pickle-tubs,
    Tables, chairs and doors;
Wormwood scrubs the public seats
    And the City Halls,
Wormwood scrubs the London streets,
    Wormwood scrubs St. Paul's.
Wormwood scrubs on her hands and knees,
    But oh, it's plainly seen
Though she use a ton of elbow-grease
    She'll never get it clean!

BLOOMSBURY

Bloomsburying! bloomsburying!
    Who will go a bloomsburying?

Down-down-with a derry-down-derrying,
Who will go a bloomsburying?
    Shovels and spades
    And birchen brooms,
    Summer is dead
    With all her blooms!
    Who will her blooms bury?
    You and I.
    Cover them up
    Where they do lie.
Bloomsburying! bloomsburying!
We must go a bloomsburying.
Down, down, with a derry-down-derrying,
We'll all go a-bloomsburying.

WILLESDEN

I went into Will's Den
    To sweep and scour and swill;
Will scowled through his spectacles
    And took it very ill.
"I'm come to turn out your dell, Will"—
    "Turn yourself out!" says Will.

ST. MARY AXE

Saint Mary, ax, Saint Mary, ax,
    Saint Mary, ax your fill,
Saint Mary, ax whatever you lacks
    And you shall have your will—
O bring me a Rose, a Christmas Rose
    To climb my window-sill—
You shall have your Rose when Heaven snows,
    Saint Mary, sleep until.

The last three poems under the heading Diversions are not from any of Eleanor Farjeon's books, but were written by her for different reasons and seem to warrant a place here. The artist, Edward Ardizzone, must have been very moved to receive a poem in gratitude for his illustrations for her collection of stories The Little Bookroom. He became her favourite illustrator.

TO TED FROM ELEANOR   September 1956

When all the fairy tales are told
And old and young go bedward,
Oh, what a debt both young and old
For ever owe you, Edward.

In darkness lit by dreams come true
The years revive their embers,
And what the child's eye saw, through you
The ageing eye remembers.

The phoenixes of infant joy
And woe and all desiring
Which time endeavours to destroy,
Arise from their first firing,

Reborn in images once born
Ere the dull brain retarded,
Picturing still our earliest morn
When words were unregarded.

So with my picture book I lie
Among the old ones bedward,
Knowing the unpaid debt which I
For ever owe you, Edward.

SERENADE TO H.G., THIRTY YEARS AFTER

My History of Hampstead tells
    How some young people, six or seven,
Serenaded H.G.Wells
    In Nineteen-Hundred-and-Eleven,
When he, those thirty years ago,
Lived in beautiful Church Row.

A summer night. We laughed and talked:
    A witty actor—and a hearty
Doctor—two sisters, girls who walked
    In beauty: we had had a party.
Light-hearted, irresponsible,
We wandered home to midnight's bell.

The very moonlight smelled of flowers.
    One of us had a concertina.
Never was merrier mood than ours.
    The genial doctor, long who'd been a
Friend of the fellow, cried with glee—
"I say! Let's serenade H.G.!"

There underneath the trees we stood
    Facing the delicate Georgian fanlight,
And as the "squiffer's" cockney mood
    Wakened the silence, we began light
Mock-Florentinian airs, sweet spells
To rouse the soul of H.G.Wells.

He would not be aroused. The stars
    Looked down on our unheeded folly,
While he foreshadowed future wars
    Or sketched another Mr.Polly.
Unthanked we stood and sang and played,
And Time drank up our serenade.

But Time has its revenges. Even
    Now, in an hour not made for laughter,

But with a moon still bright in heaven
    And flowers on earth thirty years after,
While Church Row's belfry rings its bells—
I serenade you, H.G. Wells!

Hampstead. October 1941

GATHER UP YOUR LITTER

Oranges are jolly things growing on the trees.
But on the grass their golden rings entirely fail to please,
And when you've had your revel with the luscious fruit of
        Seville,
Don't let the folk who follow sigh "Alas!"
Have some fellow feelings about your orange peelings,
And do gather up your litter from the grass.

Bananas are delightful fruit, growing in a clump,
But beauty's not their strongest suit when Mother Earth's
        their dump,
And when you're a partaker of Canary or Jamaica
Don't leave a trail behind you as you pass.
The eye with sorrow lingers on those empty yellow fingers
So do gather up your litter from the grass.

Paper can be magic fare printed on a sheet,
But when it's scattered here and there its charm is apt to
        fleet,
And when the paper's greasy, and ham sandwichy and
        cheesy,
Don't spoil the scene for every lad and lass.
Your favourite serial story will by then have lost its glory
So do gather up your litter from the grass.

Chocolate is lovely stuff as child and man have found,
But after you have had enough don't chuck the tin-foil
        round;

And when you have made merry with your Fry and your
    Cadbury
Remember that a crumpled tinsel mass
Is a feeble decoration to a flowery situation,
And do gather up your litter from the grass.

Bottles have attractions great before the corks are drawn,
But in a cracked and empty state they don't improve the
    lawn,
And after you've got busy with a drink of something fizzy,
Don't leave behind a lot of empty glass.
It's apt to prove a danger to the unsuspecting stranger,
So do gather up your litter from the grass.

(Written in 1937 for music by Martin Shaw)

THE GATE IN THE WALL

MORNING LIGHT

How beautiful! how beautiful!
　　The dew is on the grass,
And all the roses' cups are full,
　　They spill it as they pass.

The sun is very bright, and yet
　　The morning has no heat,
The pebbled path is silver-wet,
　　And oh, the air smells sweet!

It is as though I never smelt
　　So sweet and fresh an air,
It is as though I never felt
　　Such sunlight in my hair,

Or saw a diamond cobweb hang
　　Its curtain on my door,
Or ever heard the bird that sang
　　That lovely song before—

As though I saw, smelt, felt and heard
　　This morning in their prime
The web, the sun, the air, the bird,
　　And all for the first time.

THE FIRST BLACKBIRD

I've heard him, my first blackbird,
Practising at seven
Smatterings of phrases
That in May he raises
In his leafy heaven
Turning all these stray
Fragments into praises
Of the breaking day.

Mist hung like a curtain
Across the breaking day
There was scarcely light enough
To stir a bird to song,
It would not be bright enough
All the morning long
To make the blackbird certain
That Spring was on its way.

Yet there he was, my blackbird,
Whistling like a lover
Little phrases, thrilling
Once again my willing
Memory to recover
In his broken lay
All our English song birds trilling
In the breaking day.

A DRAGONFLY

When the heat of the summer
Made drowsy the land,
A dragonfly came
And sat on my hand,
With its blue jointed body
And wings like spun glass,
It lit on my fingers
As though they were grass.

KINGFISHER

A flicker of blue
Under the sallows—
Over the shallows
A kingfisher flew!

GOSSAMER

To-day I broke a lovelier thing
Than the most precious piece of Ming,
Tore a design of airier grace
Than any scrap of Mechlin Lace,
Pulled down a pile more marvellous
Than Gothic monks have left for us,
Destroyed a craft more exquisite
Than any silver-worker's bit
Of ancient art, no fine-blown glass
That which I shattered could surpass,
Cellini would have given his ears
Could he, by labouring for years,
Have been by curious toil delivered
Of what to-day at dawn I shivered.

Artist! had you not hung before
The opening of my garden-door
Your masterpiece stretched taut on air,
That silver web would still be there.

KESTREL

Still hangs the kestrel there
High in the still air
When the day is fair.

So still he seems to stay
He might in the fair day
Be fixed there far away.

But presently he will
Swoop from his airy hill
And make some small bird still.

POPPIES

Cold reigns the summer, and grey falls the day,
The flame of the year is smouldering away,
But here in the hedgerow and yonder in the wheat
The flame of the poppy is throwing out its heat.

Small grows the corn and scant is the yield
Of the hay lying strewn upon the stubble field,
But there in the meadow and here by the road
The red poppy glows as in other years it glowed.

Sunrise comes chilly and sunset comes wet,
And low burns the flame where the sun rose and set,
But red as the flame of a dawn that will not pass
The fire of the poppy is lighted in the grass.

THE WHITE BLACKBIRDS

Among the stripped and sooty twigs of the wild-cherry tree
Sometimes they flit and swing as though two blossoms of
    the Spring
Had quickened on these bleak October branches suddenly.

They are like fairy birds flown down from skies which
    no-one knows,
Their pointed yellow bills are bright as April daffodils,
Their plumy whiteness heavenly as January snows.

Loveliest guests that choose our garden plot for loitering!
Oh, what a sudden flower of joy is set upon the hour
When in their cherry cages two white blackbirds sit and
    swing.

THE GARDEN IN THE DARK

The moonlight that is neither light nor dark
Has stolen the garden's yellows, blues and reds;
The giant poplar now seems twice its mark
Reared up against the sky above the beds;
The stirless air
Seals shapeless groves of leaves no longer green;
Only on the young apple there
The clusters of the blossom, with a sheen
Pallid as moth-wings, float upon the eye
As though they had no contact with their tree,
And might at any moment rise and fly
Back to some distant star I cannot see.

POPLARS AT NIGHT

There are no trees so eloquent with wind
As poplars in the moon-mist of the dusk
When like a spirit that has slipt the husk
Among their heavenly crests its breath is thinned.

Their talk is of such high strange mysteries
They must commune in whispers lest weak men
Ere they are ripe for knowledge snatch again
The secret God has given to the trees.

EVENING HUSHES

Evening hushes
The thoughts of the Poplars
The dreams of the Rushes.

BURNING THE GATE

We're burning up the old blue garden gate,
The little gate as old as dead Queen Anne,
That stood between the small ground and the great,
The garden of the master and the man.

After two centuries the blue gate stumbled
Betwixt its posts, and hung and swung askew,
The slats were worm-eaten, the paint was crumbled,
And it must be replaced by something new.

The angry hand that pushed it is forgotten.
The tender, hesitating hand about
Its latch was dust before the latch was rotten—
Now even those old touches are burnt out.

Yes, now the flame is turning it to ash,
All goings and all comings by its way
Are smoking up the chimney, and in a flash
Of fire wipes out two centuries in a day.

THE GATE IN THE WALL

The blue gate in the wall,
The small blue gate is gone
And I alone know all
That was once seen beyond the thick
Barrier of new brick.
There was a paved walk, long
And narrow,
Where the small throng
Of saxifrages green
Crept in between
The cracks. There was a barrow
Half-full of withered flowers;
A pear tree; and a bush of silver broom;

And in that open room,
When there were sunny hours,
A graceful lady walked,
With hair as snowy as the pear-tree bloom,
And voice that always talked
As from a little distance. She
Was gone before the blue gate went from me.

But I shall see
Often through this new brick
What other eyes will not be quick
Enough to see:
The lady who once moved
Tending the beds and borders that she loved,
Whose work was never done,
Now in the early morning, now the late
Warm afternoon, but always touched with sun,
Wandering in the air
Of other summers, through the small blue gate
That is no longer there.

THE ENDING OF THE YEAR

HALLOWE'EN

On Hallowe'en the old ghosts come
About us, and they speak to some,
To others they are dumb.

They haunt the hearts that love them best;
In some they are by grief possessed,
In other hearts they rest.

They have a knowledge they would tell;
To some of us it is a knell,
To some a miracle.

They come unseen and go unseen;
And some will never know they've been,
And some know all they mean.

NOW! SAYS TIME

Now! says Time
and lifts his finger,
and the leaf on the lime
may not linger.
When Time says
Now! and lifts
his finger, the oak-leaf flutters
and drifts,
and elm and beech
let a leaf from the bough
when, finger lifted, to each
Time says *Now!*

THE OLD MAN SWEEPS THE LEAVES

The Old Man sweeps the leaves
Fallen everywhere
Through the soft cool air.
Each shake of wind bereaves
Some bough, and leaves it bare.

The gutters of old eaves
Are clogged with them, the feet
Of passers in the street
Shuffle the rustling sheaves
To chatter shrill and sweet.

The earth her own receives,
The layered hordes have flowed
Thick on the woodland road,
And time the burden weaves
Into one matted load.

And children go to school
And none of them believes
In the bare tree, or grieves
To see how in the cool
The Old Man sweeps the leaves.

THE BONFIRE

This cloud of smoke in other hours
Was leaves and grass, green twigs and flowers.

This bitter-sweet dead smell that blows
Was once the breathing of the rose.

Shapeless the forms of petals fair
And slender leaves melt on the air,

And in a scent she never knew
In life, the rose departeth too.

THE ENDING OF THE YEAR

When trees did show no leaves,
    And grass no daisies had,
And fields had lost their sheaves
    And streams in ice were clad,
And day of light was shorn,
    And wind had got a spear,
Jesus Christ was born
    In the ending of the year.

Like green leaves when they grow
    He shall for comfort be;
Like life in streams shall flow
    For running water He;
He shall raise hope like corn
    For barren fields to bear,
And therefore He was born
    In the ending of the year.

Like daisies to the grass
    His innocence he'll bring;
In keenest winds that pass
    His flowering love shall spring;
The rising of the morn
    At midnight shall appear,
Whenever Christ is born
    In the ending of the year.

THAMES IN DECEMBER

No speck, no leaf, no weedy green
Lies on the river, still and clean;
Only reflected images
Fall into it of naked trees,
Pollards whose stripped and bunchy ranks
Stand up like brooms upon the banks.

Their autumn work is finished. They
Have swept the debris all away;
The drifting flower, the drifting boat,
Green scum, white swan, no longer float
Upon the river's polished floor.
The handmaid of the year gives o'er.

The house of Thames untenanted
Stands waiting for the boisterous tread
Of scatter-brained untidy Spring,
Who, spilling as he comes, will fling
Litter of birds and flowers and men
On the disordered world again.

PLEDGES ON THE SNOW

When the air is chill,
And all is still, so still,
And Hampstead Ponds are silver sheets and white is
      Hampstead Hill,
With a child I know
Over the hills I'll go
Into the new-created world to find untrodden snow.

We'll leave to sliding boys
The Whitestone Water's joys,
We'll leave to sledding crowds the slopes, and past the

realm of noise
Somewhere out of range
We'll find a place as strange
As the first snowdrifts of the world before there came a
    change.

By crested tree and hedge
We two will trace the edge
Of many a sign our forerunners have left there for
    a pledge,
The print of foot and claw
That, travelling whitened shaw
And held, were made upon the way by them
    we never saw.

And they who left them, where
Are they? We cannot share
Ourselves with them, we gaze ahead upon the
    shapeless air,
Only underfoot
Feather and pad and boot
Walk softly softly still the level plain and knotty root.

Bird we shall never see,
Child who will never be,
Dog that will never run and leap for joy of her or me,
We whom you never knew
Go to discover too
Some white and virgin solitude and leave some pledge
    for you.

SNOWFALL

Oh, that first dazzled window-glance!
Oh, that first fall of freshest snow!
Is it a new world come by chance
Or still the old world children know?

Where is the grass and where's the road?
How everything has changed out there!
The bush is moulded by its load,
The tree is carved upon the air.

It is as though the house last night
Moved through the darkness travelling
Into a magic morn of white
While nobody felt anything:

A morn all clear and crisp that rose
Upon a land all strange and still,
A morn where ice and silence froze
The land into a trance, until

A boy with a delighted shout
The crystal of that trance shall break,
And, to its promise rushing out,
Startle all the snow awake.

THE CHILDREN'S CAROL

Here we come again, again, and here we come again,
Christmas is a single pearl swinging on a chain,
Christmas is a single flower in a barren wood,
Christmas is a single sail on the salty flood,
Christmas is a single star in the empty sky,
Christmas is a single song sung for charity.
Here we come again, again, to sing to you again,
Give a single penny that we may not sing in vain.

MUSIC AT NIGHT

I cannot hear a simple Christmas song
   Played in the night on instruments unseen
But sleeping memories awake to throng
   My sense, and the experience between

Childhood and me sinks back into the soil
   It sprang from, like a seed that has not flowered,
And consciousness no longer has in toil
   The life which it has scarred but left unsoured.

When that far music mingles with the air,
   And on my spirits sets the olden spells
Of infancy which made it strange and rare,
   If this is memory and nothing else

What else was that strange dream of infancy,
   Which full of wonder made the unconscious sense
Hear angels in the night, but memory
   Waking beyond the child's experience?

SHALL I TO THE BYRE GO DOWN?

Shall I to the byre go down
   Where the stalled oxen are?
Or shall I climb the mountain's crown
   To see the rising star?
Or shall I walk the golden floor
   Where the King's feast is spread?
Or shall I seek the poor man's door
   And ask to break his bread?

It matters not. Go where you will,
   Kneel down in cattle stall,
Climb up the cold and starlit hill,
   Enter in hut or hall,

To the warm fireside give your cheek,
    Or turn it to the snow,
It matters not; the One you seek
    You'll find where'er you go.

His sandal-sole is on the earth,
    His head is in the sky,
His voice is in the baby's mirth
    And in the old man's sigh,
His shadow falls across the sea,
    His breath is in the wind,
His tears with all who grieve left He,
    His heart with all who sinned.

Whether you share the poor man's mite
    Or taste the king's own fare,
He whom you go to seek tonight
    Will meet you everywhere;
For He is where the cattle wend,
    And where the planets shine—
Lo, He is in your eyes! Oh, friend,
    Stand still, and look in mine.

THE THIRD JOYFUL MYSTERY

    To the Manger came
All simpleness and poverty with the Shepherds,
All wisdom and all riches with the Kings,
All houselight in a single floating wick,
All eternal light in a single Star,
All lowliness in the voices of the field-beasts,
All holiness in the voices of the Angels'
    Hosanna in the Highest
All there is of Fatherhood in Heaven
    And Motherhood on earth
Were in that one small chamber of the Birth.

THE SONG OF THE FIR

There was a fir
Within a wood,
Far away, far away:
It stands no longer where it stood.
Dance around the tree today.

It had a scent
Made sweet the air,
Far away, far away:
The sweetness is no longer there.
Breathe the sweetness as you play
And dance around the tree today.

It grew between
The earth and sky,
Far away, far away:
The tree has lost its liberty
And between four walls must stay,
Breathe the sweetness as you play
And dance around the tree today.

On its tip
It bore a cone,
Far away, far away:
Now that simple fruit is gone
Hang the tree with presents gay
Mid the walls where it must stay,
Shedding sweetness where you play,
And dance around the tree today.

THE MOTHER'S TALE

Just before bed,
"Oh, one more story,
Mother!" they said
And in the glory
Of red and gold
Beyond the fender
Their Mother told
Splendour on splendour.

A small boy threw
A handful of seeds,
And a beanstalk grew
Faster than weeds
As high as heaven…
She wore a red hood…
Once there were seven
Dwarfs in a wood…

So the children found
A gingerbread house…
So Puss with a bound
Killed the Giant-mouse…
"Now, Mother, tell a
Best tale of all"
So Cinderella
Went to the ball…

"Don't stop, Mother!"
It's time to rest.
"Oh, tell us another,
The *very* best!"
So the best of all
She told to them:
"Once in a stall
In Bethlehem…"

A WISH

A glad New Year to all—
Since many a tear,
Do what we can, must fall,
A greater need to wish a glad New Year.

Since lovely youth is brief
O girl and boy,
And no-one can escape a share of grief,
I wish you joy.

Since hate is with us still
I wish men love,
I wish, since hovering hawks still strike to kill,
The coming of the dove.

And since the ghouls of terror and despair
Are still abroad,
I wish the world once more within the care
Of those who have seen God.

THE TIRED TREE

In the soft earth
   The tips already show:
Green bulbs and spears and slips
   Promising oh
Such yellow daffodils,
   Tulips so bright,
Snowdrops with double frills
   Of green and white,
Crocus of mauve and gold,
   And scylla blue,
Unfolding as of old,
   And always new.

And pushed aside, forgot,
    A tiny tree
In its December pot
    Still here I see.
Its needles dusty are,
    Its silver chain
And tarnished tinsel star
    Past use again.
How tawdry you appear,
    Small tree, today,
While knob and spire and spear
    Grow green and gay;
Yet children who, for glee
    Of flowers, cry "Oh"!
Cried "Oh"! at you, tired tree,
    A month ago.
Come, I'll undress you now,
    Your hour is dead;
I will unwind each bough
    Of silver thread,
For knob and spear and spire
    Shine in the sun,
And you must to my fire—
    The party's done.

MORNING HAS BROKEN

MORNING HAS BROKEN

Morning has broken
Like the first morning,
Blackbird has spoken
Like the first bird.
Praise for the singing,
Praise for the morning,
Praise for them, springing
Fresh from the Word.

Sweet the rain's new fall
Sunlit from heaven,
Like the first dewfall
On the first grass.
Praise for the sweetness
Of the wet garden,
Sprung in completeness
Where His feet pass.

Mine is the sunlight,
Mine is the morning,
Born of the one light
Eden saw play.
Praise with elation,
Praise every morning,
God's re-creation
Of the new day!

WE MAY NOT SAY WE LOVE

We may not say we love,
    We may a little look it,
And if he then not move
    Pretend that he mistook it:
And greet him just the same

"Good even" and "Good morrow"
And save our skin some shame,
    Though spare our heart some sorrow.
We may not walk the open way
    Though we may run the crooked—
"I love" is what we must not say
    Even when we look it.

SATURDAY NIGHT

At first was the time when the silence was only a little
And the hope of his letter kept every day alight,
And every time that the post did not bring the letter
The next time burned more bright.

Now is the time when the silence has been so long
That hope does not come with the postman to the door.
I listen still, but I've stopped expecting his letter,
I don't hope any more.

And soon the time will be that will bring me his letter
Explaining quite simply why the silence was so,
Or perhaps it will be explained by another letter,
But in any case I shall know.

But tomorrow's the day of rest, tomorrow is Sunday,
When I cannot fear for the worst or hope for the best.
There are no letters to listen for on Sunday,
Tomorrow I can rest.

A PRAYER

Lord of valleys and of trees,
Lord of hills and flowers and seas,
Lord of thunder, wind and light,
Of singing birds and birds in flight;
Lord of stars and sheep and rain,
Lord of children and of men,
Lord! I thank Thee on my knees
For blessing me with love of these.
Thou hast given me such store
I know not how to ask Thee more—
Yet once before I die, oh bless
My life that never loving less,
I need not bear Thy great excess,
Lord of Love, in loneliness!

ONE DAY

This was a day even among these days
Too full for praise;
I'll tell you what it held now it is gone,
But cannot speak thereon.
Crab apples found at sunrise washed in dew,
And sweet all through;
Birds at last plainly pairing—look and hark!—
The chaffinch and the lark;
First daisies in the grass; first celandine;
The slender lines
Of one young willow spotted with buds of white
Shining against the light
Blue heaven like a maiden's beads of prayer;
A friend to share
The day; raw cider mounting to the head;
A hot new loaf of bread;
Much foolish laughter, and much talk on things

That spread their wings
And fly beyond the boundaries of speech,
Leaving the heart to reach
The regions where the tongue can nothing say.
The end of the day
In the grey starlight of a day so full
Of stars it dropped one in a muddy pool.

TO D.B.

Do not be sad for a day that seems swiftly ended.
Nothing can end
Days that have been so perfectly befriended
By friend and friend.
For their perfection was neither of time nor of place
Nor of any weather
Or mood that brightened or shadowed this little space
Of being together.
It has been a cupful of time dipped out of an endless
Sea; it has been
A handful of earth that might have been fruitless and
        friendless,
And love made green.
What was begun in time and space is unfinished;
There is no end,
And the sea is unemptied, the earth is undiminished
For friend and friend.

THE NEED

Lord, thou who gave me all I have,
My mind's delight, my body's power,
All that in coming to the grave
I must let fall like summer's flower,
One thing Thou didst to me accord
I still shall keep: my need of Thee, O Lord.

Thou didst that everlasting gift
Upon my cradled sleep bestow,
That I in life might never lift
My head, might nothing do or know
Which in itself could perfect be
Unless, O Lord, I turned my face to Thee.

No joy wherein Thou hast no part,
Nor Love but Thou the soul of it,
Nor grief that shuts Thee from its heart,
Nor suffering that can Thee omit;
From these, if Thou be absent, I
To Heaven in my need of Thee must cry.

So even, from my coffined sleep,
When I awake, the single thing
Which I among thy gifts may keep
Shall carry me upon its wing
Into Thy presence where Thy Word
At last shall fill my need of Thee, O Lord.

PERFECT REST

More lovely than the noonday rest
In summer heat
When the warm earth gives every guest
A welcome sweet,
Is that content by which I am possessed
When I am laid at my Creator's feet.

More wonderful than rest at night
When heaven charms
Slumber with spells whose starry light
Allays alarms,
Is that repose which covers sense and sight,
When I am held in my Creator's arms.

More perfect than the ease can be
When old ones rest,
Or than the sleep of infancy
Before life's test,
Is that last breath of peace that falls on me
When I am cast on my Creator'd breast.

NOTES

1 CHILDHOOD'S FLICKERING SHADOW

The poems in this section relate to happenings and memories in Eleanor Farjeon's own childhood, as well as those of her nieces and nephew and the children of her friends. Her autobiography *A Nursery in the Nineties* gives the clue to several poems. The young Nellie Farjeon was a nervous child, with night-time fears. She is easily recognisable as the child in 'A Drink of Water', and in that poem and others she draws on the situations readers of all ages will understand. Children and adults know about being frightened during party games like "Hide and Seek," or hesitant about walking alone in a strange place.

She often wrote of her niece, Joan, daughter of her second brother Joe. One collection of Poems was titled *Joan's Door*. As well as in the named poems here, I think Joan appears in that evocative, haunting poem 'The Other Child', where she subtly admits to imagining the child she never had, the child who was "always there".

Eleanor herself is Griselda in the poem of that name. It was well-known that she greatly enjoyed her food, especially as she grew older. Her friend Denys Blakelock recalled, "Eleanor told me she was a *gourmet* and confessed to me that she had also been a *gourmande*." She looked upon this as one of the weaknesses she must watch when she became a Catholic and began thinking along more spiritual lines. The poem was set to music by the American singer and composer Nathalie Merchant in 2010.

The poems 'Bronwen' and 'Myfanwy' are named for Edward Thomas's two daughters. It was Bronwen Thomas who was shocked at this friend of their father being so ignorant about wild flowers, and took it on herself to correct this. Eleanor Farjeon grew very close to Myfanwy, the younger daughter. In 1999 Myfanwy Thomas, then 89, showed me the copy of a letter that Eleanor Farjeon had sent her in 1953. It began *Dear Polly Parrot* and was signed, from *Cocky Peacock*, their pet names for each other chosen at their long ago first meeting in 1912.

The boy in 'In Goes Robin' is Robin Guthrie, the youngest son of the artist, James Guthrie. It was Edward Thomas who introduced her to his friend Guthrie, an introduction that led to a life-long friendship. The Guthries lived at Flansham, near Bognor in Sussex, and John, Stuart and Robin were fearless sea bathers.

I have not discovered who 'Ned' is in the poem of that name, but the unusual boy's name of 'Carol', described as sounding like *a rolling car* in 'Boys' Names' is the American poet, Robert Frost's son, Carol Frost. In *Edward Thomas: the Four Last Years* she recalls him in Dymock in 1914 "*picking fruit with tireless care from morning to night for sheer love of doing it...in his absorption Carol seemed to be the very embodiment of Robert's apple-picking poem.*"

'Boys' Names' was set to music by John Ireland, 'Light the Lamps Up, Lampligher' by Harry Farjeon and 'The Old Man's Toes' by Stephen Wilkinson.

'It Was Long Ago' remains one of the best-loved, most often anthologised of all her poems. She herself could equally well be the little girl, or the old lady sitting under the tree with the cat. It is most likely that she was both.

The theme of childhood remained important throughout Eleanor Farjeon's writing. She believed, as she wrote in one story, "*in a life kept always young,*" and recording a speech for the acceptance of the Catholic Library Association's Regina Medal in April 1959 she closed with the words: "*I knew—I know—that Childhood is one of the states of Eternity, and in that state we came, we shall return.*"

2 THE TIDE IN THE RIVER

'The Night Will Never Stay' (the poem ending this section) was first published in 1920 in a book called *Gipsy and Ginger*, a quirky love story set in London, drawing on many London place names and characters. I discovered this poem handwritten across two pages of her small 1919 diary, as if it had just occurred to her. (See the reproduction printed earlier.) It is one of her most frequently quoted and anthologised poems, and deservedly so being a perfect example of a poet's skill with words, short, succinct and memorable. The final line, *"Like sorrow or a tune"*, inspired the title of this anthology.

The opening poem of this section, 'The Tide in the River' also first appeared in *Gipsy and Ginger*. The poems that follow are arranged in a time sequence, drawing on the events and people in her life between 1911 and 1918. I feel they read movingly placed in the correct order.

A few sonnets appeared in 1918 in a collection called *Sonnets & Poems*, but the entire set of sonnets which include 'First Love', 'Second Love' and a middle section called 'Interim' were not published until 1947.

Based on information from her publisher at OUP, John Bell, it became known that the subject of her "first love" was the writer, painter and entertainer, Stacy Aumonier. He was married to the pianist, Gertrude Peppercorn and I think it unlikely he knew of her feelings.

The sonnets of 'Second Love' are written to Edward Thomas and some of these show a marked change in her writing, and the earlier, almost Victorian style, is exchanged for a more natural, immediate approach.

While some of these sonnets are forgotten today, the last three of the thirteen are frequently included in anthologies of First World War poetry. In June 1947 she sent two of them to her friend Walter de la Mare, saying: *"Dearest Jack, I'd like you to have these for what they are worth. The last thirteen are Edward's."* Replying four days later he told her, *"They are sovereign sonnets, full of truth and beauty, fidelity of mind and the wisdom that comes of being all one is and trying to fit it into words."*

D.H. Lawrence had asked her to type up an article for him, grateful for her assistance in typing his novel *The Rainbow*. Her friend, Viola Meynell had first embarked on that task and called on Eleanor for help. She and Lawrence got on well with each other; their memorable walk through Sussex is documented in *The Last Four Years* (pp134-9).

She and Lawrence got on well with each other; he responded to her literary knowledge, her vitality and warm friendship. He will have found, as many did, that when you were with her she gave you her complete interest and concentration, making you feel you were her most important friend.

Although knowing he would be critical, she sent Lawrence some of the Sonnets. He responded saying *"I think there is real poetry in them."* But he accused her of holding back her strong feelings, telling her ..." *never the last dregs of bitterness will you drink, never face the last embrace of the fire."*

In poems like 'The Reflection', 'A Mother to her Daughter' and 'The Outlet' she allows her inner feelings to be known. They are amongst her most revealing work. She was devoted to her mother, Margaret (always known as Maggie). The closeness floundered when Maggie grew concerned over her daughter's friendship with Edward Thomas, who was *'a married man'*. On one occasion Maggie's concern prevented Eleanor from sharing his 37th birthday in Steep, yet her mother enjoyed his visits to their Fellows Road house, and allowed the address to be used for his correspondence with publishers.

3 THE GIFT OF ENGLISH WORDS

Some of the poems here are taken from a sequence called 'A School Child's Alphabet'. Eleanor Farjeon was attracted to the idea of using 'A to Z' as the basic structure for many of her ideas. Twenty-six stories make up a book called 'Perkin the Pedlar', and in 'Poetry' she also published: 'A Town Child's Alphabet'; 'A Country Child's Alphabet' (these two illustrated by David Jones and William Michael Rothenstein); 'An Alphabet of Magic' (illustrated by Margaret Tarrant); 'The Seaside Child's Alphabet' (illustrated by Rosalind Thornycroft). I have chosen from amongst these books some poems which show her intense love of words and literature. In the Foreword to her book 'The Little Bookroom' was this paragraph:

In the home of my childhood there was a room we called THE LITTLE BOOKROOM. True, every room in the house could have been called a bookroom. Our nurseries upstairs were full of books. Downstairs my father's study was full of them. They lined the dining-room walls and overflowed into my mother's sitting room, and up into the bedrooms. It would have been more natural to live without clothes than without books. As unnatural not to read as not to eat.

While it is not certain that Edward Thomas's poem 'Words' with its final line, *"Choose me, you English words"*, influenced her poem 'English', it seems more than likely.

4 ROOM FOR ANOTHER ONE

Eleanor Farjeon was well-known for her love of animals, especially cats. There were always cats walking on the cobbles outside her Hampstead cottage, sitting by the blue front door or sunning themselves on the walls. She once told fellow writer, Rumer Godden who had come to tea, *"I have brought a hundred and twenty-seven kittens into the world."*

'Mrs Malone' remains among her best loved poems, frequently anthologised and broadcast on radio. It was first published in 1951, and also came out, as a single poem small book, illustrated by her favourite illustrator Edward Ardizzone. In the August of that year the congregation at St. James's Church, Spanish Place, was amazed to hear the priest who received her into the Roman Catholic faith quote the lines:

> *There's room for another*
> *One, Mrs Malone.*

Many of her friends, as well as her family, identify her as

the old lady, Mrs Malone, in her generosity and welcoming of all lame dogs, whether animal or human, although she was never sad and needy like this character. Ardizzone said that he based his illustrations on her; she would have been about 70 at the time of publication, plump and very short-sighted.

The cat in 'The Golden Cat' is a mixture of several "golden" cats she had over many years. *Marmalade* or *Golden* were her favourites "…*We don't like "ginger"*, she would say. In a rather strange book called *Golden Coney* she writes of herself as "the woman", her partner George Earle (Pod) as "the man". This curious tale follows the movements of the human characters from the Hampstead cottage to one in Sussex, describing the rather erotic love-lives of the cats, based on her own Bunny, Honey, Pickle and Coney.

'The Golden Cat' has deserved more notice. It is a skilled, controlled piece of writing, leading to its inevitable ending. She winds into the poem the description of her cottage casement window, which is also described, in prose, in her rather odd story, *Golden Coney*:

One of the woman's brightest memories was of Honey running up the slope over the stairway, to poise and gather himself behind one of the open casements, and leap in a curve of light over the netting into the sunlit air. It was a movement as beautiful as anything in Nature. She thought of Greek boys playing at Kotabos, of the wine springing from the goblet in a golden arc before it rang into the waiting bowl. Or of Nijinsky, the winged rose rising incredibly through a moonlit window and vanishing in a dream. Or of the kingfisher's gleam, so bright, so swift…

'Coney, My Kitten' has not been published before. I discovered it on a crumpled typed page amongst some of Eleanor Farjeon's papers. She writes from experience; her untidy room and untidy desk will have been a happy hunting ground for a playful kitten.

5 DIVERSIONS

A great deal of Eleanor Farjeon's writing, especially in poetry, comes under the heading Diversions, and the word also happens to be the title of one of her brother Bertie's West End revues. As a family, all four Farjeons could turn their hands and pens to a wide variety of styles and subjects. Those who think of her only as a writer of Children's Stories and Poems have missed out on the witty humorous, journalistic and political writing that she published under different pseudonyms.

Again in this section you will discover that she leant on her favourite pattern of 'A to Z', and I have selected from various Alphabets. The 'ABC of the BBC' was published in 1928, which was a busy year for her. The verses are light-hearted and affectionate. She loved her wireless listening and would give friends and family instructions not to disturb her when a special programme was broadcast. Copies of 'ABC of the BBC' are hard to find nowadays. Wendy Cope explored the idea for today's listeners in a programme for BBC Radio 4's Adventures in Poetry, directed by Julian May in 2008. I think Eleanor Farjeon would have enjoyed such alternatives as 'A for Archers'.

I have included an explanatory note before the following ten poems written by Eleanor Farjeon under the pseudonym *Tomfool*. She wrote for the Daily Herald for over ten years, and readers would look out for whatever political, social, theatrical or odd piece of news would be turned and twisted into verse by the cunning hand of the anonymous jester. She had an eye for the odd, the unexpected; would seize on a hackneyed saying such as *dead as a door-nail* or *for two pins* and fit it into an unexpected scenario.

At the same time she was the anonymous *Chimaera* writing monthly poems for Time & Tide, a journal for well-read, intelligent women interested in Social Life, Culture, Politics and the Arts, under the auspices of Lady Rhonnda.

Also for Time & Tide she wrote 26 very clever, witty poems, again using 'A to Z' to advertise the excellence of the

113

magazine and encourage new readers. Each letter became a human reader, so, "Eloquent E Enlarged upon us…; Q Quoted us…; V versified our Virtues," etc. *Chimaera*'s poems were illustrated by the acclaimed artist, Gwen Raverat.

Farjeon also wrote as *Merry Andrew* for The Labour Leader, and more research is being undertaken about her writing for left-wing papers and journals, and her concerns for those who suffered through War and upheavals such as the General Strike. It has only recently been realised that she was one of the foremost writers in this field; the convention of using pseudonyms hiding her identity.

While the poem about Cricket, 'The Dull Side of Things' *was* a *Tomfool* entry, the following poem 'The Game That's Never Done' was written with her brother, Bertie Farjeon for his cricket anthology, now a collector's item, in 1946. Encouraged by her brothers she developed a love of the game, and as well as these two poems, cricket is the subject of a short story, *Spooner*.

'The Town Child's Alphabet' along with 'The Country Child's Alphabet' were commissioned by Harold Monro for publication by The Poetry Bookshop in 1924. The first was illustrated by David Jones and has become much sought after. The second, in which the poems are less inventive (and not included here) was illustrated by the then 16 year old William Michael Rothenstein.

The woman selling flowers in 'F is for Flower Seller', is known to be Maggie, famous for many years for her stall in Hampstead. The other characters, Waitress, Queue Girl, and Roadmender, are evocative of the London of the 1920s. 'J is for Jazz-Man' was set to music by Benjamin Britten.

'The Sussex Alphabet' appears unillustrated in a couple of her collections, but was also published in a large size, fully illustrated artistic publication by James Guthrie's Pear Tree Press in 1939. Sheila Thompson was the artist. It was Edward Thomas who introduced Eleanor to Guthrie, and they became devoted friends. She frequently visited the Guthrie family in Flansham, Sussex.

The poem 'All the Way to Alfriston' was published by

Guthrie's young sons on their own little Greenleaf Press, illustrated by Robin (as mentioned earlier) to show the poet on the title page. She wrote, in *The Last Four Years: "Why he chose to depict me as a sort of H.G. Wellsian tramp in check knickerbockers I could not understand, and neither, now, can he,"* (now, being 1957). With its pretty flowered print cover this small limited edition is now hard to find. Robin Guthrie became a well-known artist, and among his work is another early achievement: at 16 he made the collectable lino cut of Edward Thomas walking, reprinted in many publications and on cards.

'Nursery Rhymes of London Town'. By 1915 Eleanor Farjeon was contributing regularly to the popular magazine Punch with rhymes based on London places. They are a clear example of her gift for word play and innuendo, of looking at words, twisting them, giving them a new life, sometimes 'off-centre', sometimes absurd. As always her gift for rhyme serves her purpose. There was an expectant readership and she didn't fail. They were, it seemed, especially enjoyed by soldiers at the Front, and one young soldier, Victor Haslam, wrote to her to *"thank her for keeping his spirits up."* They corresponded, he visited her home and later she dedicated *Martin Pippin* to him before their relationship ended, leaving Eleanor very deeply affected.

The poet, Gordon Bottomley, wrote to say that his friend, Edward Thomas, had wanted him to read them, and how much he liked them. Edward Thomas told her, *"They all surprise, yet not too much, just enough to make one wish one had invented them oneself."*

For Christmas 1916 Eleanor included a new rhyme 'St. Mary Axe' with Edward Thomas's Christmas gifts and, writing to her on 27 December, he said: *"the poem is I think one of your happiest. Why do I like the last line so much? What does the "Until" remind me of? Or is it just that it reminds me of something else that is good?..."*

She set many of the Nursery Rhymes to music. Although it was her older brother, Harry Farjeon, who was the professional musician, she had the gift for setting tunes to her verses, and these are memorable. In the 1930s and 40s they were very popular in school singing classes and for concerts. *Nursery Rhymes of London Town* (1917) and later *More Nursery Rhymes* (1918) were amusingly illustrated by Macdonald Gill, in bright primary colours. Some were included in an exhibition in Brighton in 2011. It is also interesting to recall that Wallis Simpson copied 'King's Cross' into her own commonplace book, and a newspaper article cited it as her own idea. A Farjeon fan soon put this right!

'To Ted from Eleanor'. The poem was accompanied by a letter which tells the artist: "*I wasn't prepared for what you have given my book. I found my eyes filling with tears again and again. All childhood is there, all I feel about childhood, in the dim recesses where that part of me still lives. Thank you with all my heart. I wish I could do something for you. With love and gratitude....Eleanor.*" The poem was obviously her return gift.

'Serenade to H.G.' Written in 1941, she is looking back 30 years to 1911 when she and her brothers knew many young people in Hampstead, writers, actors, doctors and musicians amongst them. The hearty doctor in the poem is Godwin Baynes, who was studying under Jung at that time. The girls who "walked in beauty" were Rosalind and Joan Thornycroft, daughters of the sculptor, Sir Hamo Thornycroft and cousins of Siegfried Sassoon. Rosalind illustrated three Farjeon books; Joan married Herbert Farjeon. A "squiffer" is a concertina.

6 THE GATE IN THE WALL

Eleanor Farjeon was always fond of gardens, very conscious of weathers and seasons. In several of her poetry collections she chooses to place poems in a seasonal order. As with the "Alphabets" it seems that she is comfortable with a simple structure.

The poems here come from various selections of her poetry, written across a span of years and have been chosen to show the way she looked at the natural world. At one time she had two gardens, one in Hampstead and the other in Laughton, Sussex, and in both had help from gardeners.

'K is for Kestrel' is from the 'Country Childs' Alphabet'.

'The White Blackbirds'. A letter sent by Edward Thomas from France in July 1916 includes: *"So you have a white blackbird. Good luck to you and it. It is certain to be a white blackbird. It will have a better chance in Hampstead than ours had in Steep..."*

7 THE ENDING OF THE YEAR

Again here the change in weather and seasons have an effect on the writer, with falling leaves and the scent of bonfires marking a mood change.

Eleanor Farjeon was a great lover of any festive occasion, and loved planning and cooking and entertaining for guests, friends and family. Christmas was always special. Her non-practising Jewish father arranged the most lavish and special Christmas parties in her childhood, and something of his eagerness to give, and share, was passed on to her.

Her birthday, February 13th which she had so wished was a day later as that would have been more romantic...was always "an occasion" and she would start planning for Christmas well ahead. A collection of Christmas poems *Come Christmas*, was published in 1927 and republished by the Cyder Press at the University of Gloucestershire in 2000. Poems from that collection are included here, and some show that her religious beliefs, though perhaps based on tradition, were already important a good twenty years before her reception into the Roman Catholic Church.

The poem 'Snowfall' had a separate publication in 1928 when published as a card by the Favil Press, in Kensington, evocatively illustrated by the well-known artist, C.R.W. Nevinson.

8 MORNING HAS BROKEN

This section takes its title from the hymn that has become so well known, and its origins a subject of great interest. There has been much debate about the writing of the poem, its musical setting and the first date of publication. Among her friends were the Reverend Percy Dearmer, vicar of St. Mary the Virgin, Primrose Hill, who was involved with the composers Ralph Vaughan-Williams, and more particularly Martin Shaw, in editing *Songs of Praise*. First published in 1926, when a new enlarged edition was planned for 1931, Shaw invited Eleanor Farjeon to create new words to a traditional Gaelic tune *'Bunessan'*. She duly obliged with 'Morning has Broken' (the original tune, setting had been for the carol *'Child in the Manger'* with words by Mary MacDonald). Dearmer and Shaw felt that there was no hymn in praise of the Beginning of Day. It was sung quite often in schools and churches, but came to the fore as a popular song when Cat Stevens adapted the original tune for his 1971 album *Teaser & the Firecat.*

It will be noted that when printed in anthologies as a poem called 'A Morning Song', the words are altered, possibly to have secular rather than religious appeal. Wendy Cope, wanting to use the poem in an anthology, noticed the discrepancy. It is not known whether Eleanor Farjeon agreed to this alteration in 1941 when it appeared in her *Book of Days* for 21st March, sub-titled *For the First Day of Spring* or in a 1957 anthology called *The Children's Bells* with the same title. In *Songs of Praise* the hymn is sub-titled *Thanks for a Day*. Here we have kept to the original version. Eleanor Farjeon died before knowing of her hymn's popularity and would have been surprised to see the certificates awarded by Broadcast Music Inc for achievement as measured by over one million performances. It would have equally surprised her to have heard Roger McGough's take on her idea which he read in Radio 4's Adventures in Poetry.

MORNING HAS BROKEN....

Too late the billion gallons of sun lotion
Smeared over the earth's surface
The straw hat covering three continents
Too late the sunglasses wrapped around the equator
The giant space parasol
Too late the ozone elastoplast

Morning is broken....
Is it too late to mend it?

'We May Not Say We Love' and 'Saturday Night' are two sad poems that were written after the Great War ended. In 1999, when writing the introduction to a new edition of *Edward Thomas: The Four Last Years*, I had assumed these poems referred to Edward Thomas, but later discovering that I was wrong. They in fact refer to Victor Haslam, who is the subject of an unpublished work among Eleanor Farjeon's papers, *A Walk in the Dark*, a fictionalised story of her love for him. After the War, it seemed for a while as if they might share a future together. It was not to be.

'One Day' was originally published under *Tomfool* in the Daily Herald. Every so often in this series a serious poem would appear, and this one being especially joyous and full of praise must have offered *Tomfool's* readers an uplifting mood. It may well have been about a day that she spent with her friend, the actor Denys Blakelock, whom she first met when he played the part of King Nollekins in her play *The Silver Curlew* at the Arts Theatre, London in 1949... *"In 'Forty Nine/ A Curlew flew/And there was I/And there were You..."* she wrote to him.

If the poem 'One Day' may have been based on a day they spent together, the following poem 'To D.B.' was certainly written after such a day. It seems appropriate that a poem *he* wrote for *her* should have a place here, offering, as it does, such moving thoughts on a Friendship.

Do not be sad for a time that seems swiftly ended.
Nothing can end
Days that have been so perfectly befriended
By friend and friend.
For their perfection was neither of time nor of place,
Nor of any weather
Or mood that brightened or shadowed this little space
Of being together.
It has been a cupful of time dipped out of an endless
Sea: it has been
A handful of earth that might have been fruitless and friendless
And love made green.
What was begun in time and place is unfinished;
There is no end,
And the sea is unemptied, the earth is undiminished
For friend and friend.

The last two poems are also hymns in *Songs of Praise*. Their titles are simply 'Need' and 'Rest' and were set to music in turn by Harry Farjeon and Gordon Slater. They were written before the enlarged edition of the hymn book was published, probably in the late 1920s, and bring to mind her early sonnet *'I come to wish I could believe in God'*. She told friends that the opening line had been *most marvellously answered* when she was received into the Catholic Church.

It has not been possible to safely date every poem. A writer like Eleanor Farjeon, whose writing life spanned at least fifty years, leads her readers down many pathways. Early poems appeared in magazines and papers, emerging like new many years later. The Select Bibliography that follows attempts to list her most important poetry publications in order of their date of publication.

SELECT BIBLIOGRAPHY

1908 PAN WORSHIP AND OTHER POEMS, Elkin Matthews
1911 DREAM SONGS FOR THE BELOVED, Orpheus Press
1916 NURSERY RHYMES OF LONDON TOWN, Duckworth
1917 MORE NURSERY RHYMES OF LONDON TOWN,
    Duckworth
1918 SONNETS AND POEMS, Blackwell
1918 ALL THE WAY TO ALFRISTON, The Morland Press *for*
    The Greenleaf Press
1920 TOMFOOLERIES (*by TOMFOOL*), The Labour
    Publishing Company, (The Daily Herald)
1921 MOONSHINE (*by TOMFOOL*), The Labour Publishing
    Company, (The Daily Herald)
1921 TIME & TIDE ALPHABET (by Chimaera), Time & Tide
1922 SONGS FOR MUSIC & TUNES OF A PENNY PIPER,
    Selwyn & Blount
1923 THE YEAR ROUND, Wm. Collins
1924 THE TOWN CHILD'S ALPHABET (illust. David Jones)
    THE COUNTRY CHILD'S ALPHABET (illust. William
    Michael Rothenstein)
1925 YOUNG FOLK AND OLD, High House Press
1926 JOAN'S DOOR, (illust. Will Townsend), Wm. Collins
1927 COME CHRISTMAS (illust. Molly Arthur), Wm. Collins
    (republished by The Cyder Press, Cheltenham 2000)
1928 AN ALPHABET OF MAGIC (illust. Margaret Tarrant),
    The Medici Press
1930 THE ABC OF THE BBC (illust. T.C.Derrick), Wm. Collins
1933 OVER THE GARDEN WALL (illust. Gwen Raverat),
    Faber & Faber
1938 SING FOR YOUR SUPPER (illust. Isobel & John Morton
    Sale), Michael Joseph
1939 A SUSSEX ALPHABET (illust. Sheila Thompson), Pear
    Tree Press
1942 CHERRYSTONES (illust. Isobel & John Morton Sale),
    Michael Joseph
1945 THE MULBERRY BUSH (illust. Isobel & John Morton
    Sale), Michael Joseph

1947 FIRST AND SECOND LOVE: SONNETS, Michael Joseph
1949 THE STARRY FLOOR (illust. Isobel & John Morton Sale),
     Michael Joseph
1950 MRS MALONE (illust. David Knight), Michael Joseph
1951 SILVER–SAND AND SNOW, Michael Joseph
1957 THE CHILDREN'S BELLS (illust. Peggy Fortnum), OUP
1969 AROUND THE SEASONS (illust. Jane Paton), Hamish
     Hamilton

In Collaboration with HERBERT FARJEON
1932 KINGS AND QUEENS
1933 HEROES AND HEROINES. (illust. Rosalind Thornycroft),
     Victor Gollancz, 1983/1987 (illust. Robin Jacques), J.M
     Dent and Puffin Books
2002 KINGS & QUEENS Republished with illustrations by
     Robin Jacques, Jane Nissen Books
2011 Both books republished as facsimiles of the originals by
     The British Library

FURTHER READING

A NURSERY IN THE NINETIES, Eleanor Farjeon's Memoir of
her Childhood, Victor Gollancz 1938/1960

EDWARD THOMAS: THE LAST FOUR YEARS, Memoir of her
four year friendship with Edward Thomas, OUP 1958/1979.
Revised edition, Sutton Publishing (1997), with a Foreword by
P.J. Kavanagh and Introduction by Anne Harvey, including the
following additional material: Farjeon's forewords to Robert
Frost's YOU COME TOO (1964) and Selected Poems of
Edward Thomas: THE GREEN ROADS (1965), both first
published by The Bodley Head. This edition also includes
some Sonnets and the poem WALKING TOM by Clifford Bax
and Herbert Farjeon.

Both these important titles are available under the Faber Finds
imprint.

INDEX OF TITLES
Untitled poems are listed under their first line

ABC of the BBC	53
All the Way to Alfriston	72
Alphabet	36
Angel, The	75
Arundel	70
B is for Big Ben	53
Battersea	74
Bedtime	19
Belloc	71
Be Patient With Me	24
Blind Alley	8
Bloomsbury	76
Bonfire, The	90
Books	42
Boys' Names	17
Bravery	6
Bronwen of the Flowers	10
Burning the Gate	87
Cats	48
Certain Among Us Walk in Loneliness	25
Children's Carol, The	94
Coney: My Kitten, To	50
D.B., To	104
Dog	50
Dragonfly, A	83
Drink of Water, A	20
Dull Side of Things, The	64
Easter Monday (In Memoriam E.T.)	34
Ending of the Year, The	91
English	36
Epitaph	52

Evening Hushes	86
Exposure of the Creeps, An	63
F is for Flower Seller	67
First Blackbird, The	82
Fleet Street	76
Game That's Never Done, The	65
Garden in the Dark, The	86
Gate in the Wall, The	87
Gather Up Your Litter	80
Girls' Names	9
Golden Cat, The	48
Good Morning	3
Good Night	20
Gossamer	84
Griselda	12
Hallowe'en	89
Hammersmith	75
Here We Go Round the Mulberry Bush	16
Hide-And-Seek (Hiding)	14
Hide-And-Seek (Seeking)	15
House Coming Down	7
I Am Not Very Often Careless Now	26
I Come to Wish	28
I Have Found Friends	25
I Marvel Now in What Exalted State	24
If You Had Held Me in More Tenderness	31
Immortal Motley, The	61
In Goes Robin	18
Inside	51
It Is A Wrong to You My Friend	30
It Was Long Ago	22
J is for Jazz	54
J is for Jazz Man	67
Joan, For	12

Joan's Corner   9

Kensal Rise   75
Kestrel   84
Kingfisher   83
King's Cross   73
Knowledge   38

L is for Licence   54
Latin   38
Light The Lamps Up, Lamplighter   21
Long Man of Wilmington   71
Lullaby in Lingerie, A   61

Mary Indoors   37
Mary's One   40
Meeting Mary   9
Morning Has Broken   101
Morning Light   82
Mother's Tale, The   98
Mother to Her Daughter, A   30
Mr Sheraton's Cat   49
Mrs Malone   44
Music at Night   95
Myfanwy Among the Leaves   11

N is for News Bulletin   55
Ned   18
Need, The   105
Night Will Never Stay, The   35
Nothing   52
Now! Says Time   89
Now That You Too Must Shortly Go   30

Oh, Hark!   22
Old Man's Toes, The   4
Old Man Sweeps the Leaves, The   90
On the Snow   32
One Day   103

Ornithology   39
Other Child, The   15
Outlet, The   33
Oxford Circus   76

P is for Policeman   68
P is for Programme   56
Peace   34
Pegasus   41
Perfect Rest   106
Perfection of the Stranger, The   60
Pledges on the Snow   92
Poetry   40
Poplars at Night   86
Poppies   85
Prayer, A   103
Preferences   58

Q is for Questions   57
Q is for Queue Girl   68

R is for Roadmender   69
Random Reflections on a Park Seat   59
Ravenous Justice   62
Reflection, The   26
Reflections on Two Pins   58
Rye   71

Saturday Night   102
Serenade to H.G., Thirty Years After   79
Shadows, For   28
Shall I to the Byre Go Down?   95
Shepherd's Bush   74
Silence   28
Snowfall   94
Song of the Fir, The   97
St. Mary Axe   77
Stock Exchange, The   74

T is for Taxi-Man   69
Ted from Eleanor, To   78
Thames in December   92
There Isn't Time   4
Third Joyful Mystery, The   96
Three Miles to Penn   32
Tide in the River, The   24
Tired Tree, The   99
Tree-Law   64

U is for Uncle   69
Uckfield   71

W is for Waitress   70
Waking Up   3
We May Not Say We Love   101
When We Had Reached the Bottom of the Hill   31
When You Are By, What Things Are Said   29
White Blackbirds, The   85
Willesden   77
Wish, A   99
Wormwood Scrubs   76

Yet Sometimes Still When I Am Left Alone   26
You Seem To Me Beyond All Men to Need   29